the Kansas City Star Quilts

SAMPLER

60+ Blocks from 1928 to 1961

Historical Profiles by Barbara Brackman

Compiled by the Editors of C&T Publishing

C&T PUBLISHING

Text, photography, and artwork copyright © 2018 by C&T Publishing, Inc.

Publisher: Amy Marson

Creative Director: Gailen Runge

Acquisitions Editor: Roxane Cerda

Managing Editor: Liz Aneloski

Editorial Compiler: Gailen Runge

Project Editor: Alice Mace Nakanishi

Developmental Editors: Jenifer Dick, Edie McGinnis, and Judy Pearlstein

Technical Editors: Jane Miller, Linda Johnson, and Debbie Rodgers

Cover/Book Designer: April Mostek

Production Coordinator: Zinnia Heinzmann

Illustrators: Kirstie L. Pettersen and Linda Johnson

Photo Assistant: Mai Yong Vang

Cover/sampler quilt photography by Mai Yong Vang of C&T Publishing, Inc.; section opener quilt photography by Aaron T. Leimkuehler; profiles section photography by Jon Blumb

Published by C&T Publishing, Inc., P.O. Box 1456, Lafayette, CA 94549

Library of Congress Cataloging-in-Publication Data

Title: The Kansas City star quilts sampler : 60+ blocks from 1928 to 1961 : historical profiles / compiled by the editors of C&T Publishing.

Other titles: Kansas City star (Kansas City, Mo. : 1885)

Description: Lafayette, CA : C&T Publishing, Inc., [2018]

Identifiers: LCCN 2018030451 | ISBN 9781617456909 (soft cover : alk. paper)

Subjects: LCSH: Quilting--Kansas--History. | Patchwork quilts--Kansas. | Patchwork--Kansas--Patterns. | Quilting--Kansas--Patterns.

Classification: LCC TT835 .C348 2018 | DDC 746.46041--dc23

LC record available at https://lccn.loc.gov/2018030451

Printed in the USA

10 9 8 7 6 5 4 3 2 1

Contents

1933
Charm Quilt

1934
Red Cross

1935
Arkansas
Snowflake

1935
Railroad
Crossing

1935
Bridle Path

1935
Arabic Lattice

1936
Turkey Tracks

1936
White Lily

1937
Depression

1938
Fair and Square

1939
Hexagon Beauty

1940s 135

1940
Garden Walk

1940
Comfort Quilt

1940
Quilter's Fan

1941
Fence Row

1941
Star of Alamo

1941
Four-Leaf
Clover

1941
Radio Windmill

1942
Thorny Thicket

1942
Chain Quilt

1942
Rose Bud

1943
Evelyn's
Whirling
Dust Storm

1944
Friendship
Name Chain

1945
Scottish Cross

1946
Return of the
Swallows

1947
Little Boy's
Britches

1948
Granny's Choice

1949
Crazy Anne #2

The Commercial Quilt Network and *The Kansas City Star*

by Barbara Brackman

The history of commercial needlework patterns is a story of women's work. The Midwestern companies described here were run primarily by women who designed patterns for the newspapers, who sold patterns in department store dry goods sections, who pasted up simple mail order catalogs and folded mimeographed designs into brown paper envelopes. Needlework pattern companies were often cottage industries—small businesses run from women's homes with the help of their sisters or their husbands, their mothers or their children and an occasional paid employee.

Related to the pattern sources were the needlework columns in the newspapers and magazines of the time, an empire managed by female editors, such as Louise Roote and Edna Marie Dunn (page 42), who made their careers in the women's section, discussing fashion or cooking. Their empires, of course, may also be viewed as a ghetto. Women were generally confined to the middle pages of the magazine or the "women's section" of the newspaper. Louise Roote was one ladies' page editor fortunate enough to stay in the business until World War II, when she graduated from the women's page to become general editor at *Capper's Weekly*. Like many other wartime women, she took over a traditional man's job.

Many women found needlework patterns to be remarkably profitable. Some husband and wife teams, and women who lived without husbands to provide support, found managing a needlework company a prosperous alternative to traditional salaried occupations.

The history of quilt pattern publication in America is generally traced to an 1835 article in *Godey's Lady's Book* picturing a hexagon design. Magazines sporadically printed quilt designs between 1835 and 1880, but it isn't until late in the nineteenth century that periodicals regularly referred to quilts, mentioning the current fads such as crazy patch and embroidered redwork. In the 1890s, references continued to increase. Quilt designs became a consistent feature of the readers' exchange columns in women's and farm magazines. "Does anyone have a pattern for a Drunkard's Path?" one reader might ask, to be followed up the next month by a sketch of the block in question. These exchanges functioned much like the quilt computer lists of the twenty-first century that share patterns and techniques throughout the country.

In the early twentieth century, periodicals began selling full-sized diagrams for the patterns that readers mailed in to the editor. The woman's page might picture a block and ask readers to send a nickel or dime for the pattern. This combination of pictured block and mail-order pattern became the standard periodical format for decades. Among Ruby Short McKim's (page 10) many innovations was the idea of publishing the actual pattern to scale in the teens.

Magazine mail-order departments competed with companies devoted solely to selling designs through the mail. During the last decades of the nineteenth century, while Montgomery Wards and Sears, Roebuck and Company were taking advantage of rural free delivery to sell fabric,

batting, and quilt frames through the mail, pattern companies like the Ladies Art Company, run by H. M. Brockstedt of St. Louis, sold patterns. Brockstedt is credited with the first catalog devoted to quilt patterns, published in 1889.

The catalogs were often free, but quilters were also willing to pay a quarter for the advertising booklets, just for the chance to see photographs of blocks and antique quilts. Most seamstresses at the time had the pattern making skills to draft their own templates if they had a sketch or photo of the finished block.

In the late 1920s, newspapers around the nation responded to reader requests for a regular pattern feature. *The Star's* was among the earliest with the first appearing on September 22, 1928. Ruby McKim's design initiated a column that lasted until May 24, 1961 with the last of Edna Marie Dunn's many drawings. The pattern usually appeared in the Saturday paper and was repeated on Wednesdays in the weekly farm periodical published by *The Star*. *The Weekly Star Farmer*, also called *The Weekly Kansas City Star*, reached subscribers in Missouri, Kansas, Oklahoma, Colorado, Nebraska, Iowa, and Arkansas.

In addition to their unique full-sized pattern feature, the paper also offered two different reader mail services, syndicated pattern features for mail order designs, a new quilt pattern format. Syndicated quilt columns began in the late 1920s and within a few years dominated the periodical pattern network. *The Star* was one of a very few papers that continued to run a unique quilt column featuring regional designs after the advent of the syndicated quilt column. Most, like *Capper's Weekly* and the *Oklahoma Farmer*

Stockman (page 12), subscribed to the reader mail services operated by Needlecraft Supply (page 43), which sold designs under the name of Laura Wheeler, or Kansas City's Colonial Patterns, which used the name Aunt Martha.

The quilt revival that flourished from the late 1920s through the 1940s began to lose steam after World War II. Quilts were again perceived as part of the world of poverty, hand-me-downs, and country crafts, concepts quite unpopular in the 1950s. By 1960, most of the needlework companies were closed and the quilt columns, including *The Star*'s, were replaced with television listings and Dear Abby features.

Color: Thirties Reproductions

People commonly refer to the pastel quilts from the mid-twentieth century as "Depression Quilts," but the fashion for light clear colors in scrappy patchwork combined with a neutral of plain white cotton appeared before the 1929 stock market crash and the economic crisis of the 1930s. During the midtwenties, America was undergoing a different crisis of social changes. Women who bobbed their hair and shortened their skirts were ready to take up quiltmaking so long as the look was modern. Louise Fowler Roote, writing for *Capper's Weekly*, described the new color scheme, when she advised readers to piece an old pattern, "not in the brilliant red and green oil calico of colonial times, but in the soft pastel colorings of maize and pale green on an ivory background."

New dyes and new technology enabled fabric mills to give quilters inexpensive cottons printed in the whole spectrum of colors, a real change from the unreliable, dark cottons available through World War I. During the late 1920s, splashy prints covered with layers of stylized flowers were fresh and new. Art deco zigzags, plaids, and stripes coexisted on the same fabric with tulips, daisies, and pansies. The prints combined any number of shades, but the recurring color theme was white. The majority of the dress prints from the time and the majority of the quilts made with those fabrics include white. The quilts therefore have a light appearance, despite the dark and bright details of the colors in the prints.

Although design principles weren't often written down, we can infer a few general rules by looking at the quilts of the time. Among them:

1. Any color goes with any other color.

2. The more colors the better.

3. The neutral is white, which usually dominates the quilt's color scheme.

4. The more prints the better.

5. Contrast, rather than focusing on light and dark, balances prints versus plains.

6. Colors were clear with little interest in a toned down or grayed palette.

1920s

See the Rob Peter to Pay Paul block (page 23).

Peter, Paul, and Aunt Mary, designed by Lynda Hall of Apopka, Florida; quilted by The Olde Green Cupboard staff of Jacksonville, Florida

Ruby McKim

Needlework Trendsetter

by Barbara Brackman

Quilt pattern columns seem at home in the Kansas City area, possibly due to the innovations and influence of one woman. In 1916, 25-year-old Ruby Short collaborated with children's author Thornton Burgess to produce a series of quilt patterns in *The Kansas City Star*. The *Bed-Time Quilt* featured embroidered animals from Burgess stories outlined in rather cubistic fashion, a style McKim called "Quaddy Quilties." McKim biographer Jill Sutton Filo has speculated the strange name is a possible reference to the quadrilateral shapes of the quadrupeds. In the early 1920s, McKim's modern quilt blocks began appearing in other papers. The "Quaddy Quilties" in the *Bed-Time Quilt* are thought to be the first syndicated pattern series.

Ruby Short was born July 27, 1891, to Morris Trimble Short and Viola M. Vernon Short. Ruby's art talent was apparent even as a girl. Her adolescent drawings show the same sure hand and sense of style as her later needlework designs. Viola managed to send Ruby to art school for a time. She attended the New York School of Fine and Applied Arts (now Parsons School of Design) but did not graduate.

She returned to Independence and became a public school art teacher. Ruby soon took a position at a trade school in the Kansas City school system. While teaching, Ruby published the *Quaddie Quiltie Bed-Time Quilt*. In 1917 she married Arthur McKim, whom she'd known since childhood.

In the early 1920s, they founded McKim Studios. Arthur was in charge of the business and editorial departments, while Ruby did the designing. They syndicated quilt and needlework patterns, published pattern booklets and mail-order catalogs, and sold kits under the name McKim-Cut Quilts, while raising two girls and a boy. Quilt design, with its inexpensive patterns, was a good business when women had little to spend on their hobbies, and McKim Studios, one of the earliest of the quilt cottage industries, was quite successful.

Son Kim recalled a warm home in which all the beds "boasted a handmade quilt as the top cover." Quilts, both antique and those made in Ruby's designs, were stored in "heaping stacks," in a "big hall closet." Ruby's murals of the family at work and play covered the walls of their house in Independence.

In September 1928, Ruby launched a new series in *The Kansas City Star*. *The Pine Tree Quilt*, a traditional design, was the first of over 1,000 full-sized patterns the newspaper would print in the next three decades. She designed the weekly quilt block for *The Star* until 1930, when Eveline Foland (page 40) took over the column. Ruby's patterns were syndicated to numerous other newspapers around the country. She also wrote and designed for magazines such as *Better Homes and Gardens*, *Child Life*, and *Successful Farming*.

Most of her creative work in quilt design was finished by the time she was forty. Husband and wife decided to take their children on a trip to Europe in 1933, during the depths of the Depression when money for most families was in short supply. The quilt pattern business had been a good career choice for the McKims. During the early 1930s, Ruby's attention turned to antique dolls. She was editor of *Doll Talk* magazine for decades and the family business evolved into Kimport Dolls. Arthur died in June 1967 at 76, and Ruby followed in July 1976, a few days short of her 85th birthday.

Oklahoma Farmer Stockman
Rural Resource

by Barbara Brackman

The Weekly Star Farmer was *The Star*'s sister newspaper published for the agricultural market in the Midwest. Farm wives expected quilt patterns in their periodicals and for decades *The Star* duplicated the pattern from Sunday's city paper in Wednesday's *Star Farmer* (also called for a time the *Weekly Kansas City Star*.)

Periodicals giving news and advice to farmers date to the early nineteenth century. Agricultural papers thrived as printing technology improved, paper became cheaper, the farming population increased and mail rates dropped. It's estimated that ninety farm periodicals were published in 1870, a number that doubled in the next decade. The journals were generally regional in scope with a *New England Farmer*, a *Rural New Yorker*, and a *Western Farm Journal* catering to different climate, crops and politics. Competition dictated features for the family and many magazines had a women's page with household hints and needlework patterns.

Many of the women's pages offered fashion patterns as well as needlework and quilting designs.

Farm families on the Great Plains could subscribe to a variety of agricultural periodicals, among them the *Oklahoma Farmer Stockman*. The weekly included an original quilt pattern feature on their homemaking page, which was titled Good Cheer. In the 1920s and early 1930s, the patterns that appeared in the paper were mailed to the editors by readers from Kansas, Oklahoma, and Texas, indicating the range of households reached by the paper.

Unique pattern columns such as the Good Cheer feature are valuable to quilt pattern collectors because they recorded regional names and designs. In 1921, a woman from Kiowa County, Oklahoma, sent The Hog Pen—a Log Cabin variation more commonly known as Court House Steps. That local name was never recorded in the big city publications, possibly because Hog Pen was considered too folksy, too rural, too low-brow for a more sophisticated audience. Many of the regional subscribers, however, must have recognized the down-to-earth name.

1928 Pine Tree

Finished block: 12˝ × 12˝

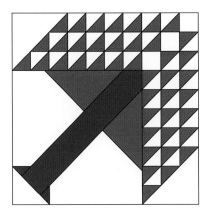

Fabric Needed

Background • Green • Brown

Cutting Instructions

Use the Pine Tree patterns (pages 16–18).

From background fabric, cut:

- 2 triangles using pattern A

- 1 each of patterns F, D, and E

- 3 squares using pattern C

- 36 triangles using pattern B

From green fabric, cut:

- 42 triangles using pattern B

- 2 triangles using pattern G

From brown fabric, cut:

- 2 triangles using pattern I

- 1 piece using pattern H

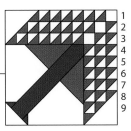

Newspaper Archive

Appeared in *The Kansas City Star* on September 19, 1928 (block #1)

The pine tree blocks make a very handsome quilt. It takes 16 pieced blocks to make a quilt about 84˝ square, aside from its border. These blocks must be set together diagonally with alternating blocks of white, cut the exact size of the pieced block. The patterns are the exact size in which the pieces should be cut. The size of one block when put together is about 15˝. Seams must be allowed in addition, for quiltmakers differ in opinion as to seam width. The best way is to trace the patterns on cardboard, mark and cut to complete your pattern. Lay the cardboard patterns on the material. The pattern is drawn with pencil carefully. Cut a seam larger, sewing on the pencil line. The 2 white pieces of irregular shape have to be fitted in as marked on the edges; otherwise the Pine Tree is largely a business of sewing triangles into squares and adding them together.

To Make the Block

1. Make half-square triangles by sewing a background B triangle to a green B triangle. Make 36 half-square triangles. Set these aside for the moment.

To make the lower part of the block, sew the brown I triangle to the background F piece. Add the green G triangle. Sew this to the brown H piece. Now sew the remaining brown I triangle to the background D piece. Add the remaining green G triangle. Sew this section to the opposing side of the tree trunk. Now sew the background E triangle to the base of the tree trunk.

2. We are now ready to make the top of the tree. Always refer to the colored diagram for color placement orientation.

For row 1, begin with a green B triangle, add 6 half-square triangle units. Finish the row with a C square.

3. Row 2, begin with a B triangle, and add half-square triangle units. Sew a C square and finish the row with a half-square triangle unit. *NOTE: The last half-square triangle unit is turned in a different direction from the rest of the row.*

4. Row 3, begin with a B triangle, add 6 half-square triangle units. Add a C square and finish the row with 2 half-square triangle units. *NOTE: The last 2 half-square triangle units are turned in a different direction from the rest of the row.*

5. Sew the 3 rows together and add a background A triangle. This is the top part of the tree. Set this aside for the moment.

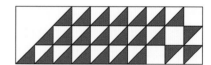

6. Rows 4–7, sew 3 half-square triangles together. Check the color orientation.

7. Row 8, sew 2 half-square triangles together. End the row with a green B triangle.

8. Row 9, sew a half-square triangle to a green B triangle.

9. Sew rows 4–9 together as shown.

10. Add the remaining green B triangle to the bottom of the rows.

11. Sew a background A triangle to the 3 rows.

12. Sew this strip to the square you've made that has the tree trunk. Now add the strip made up of the first 3 rows to the top to finish the block.

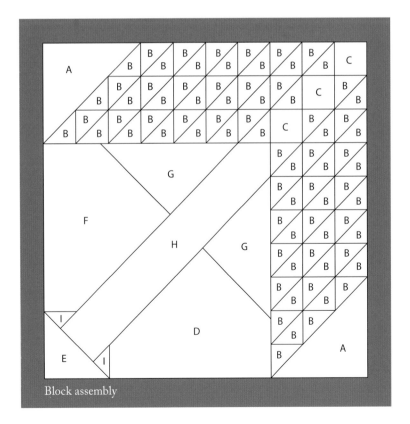

Block assembly

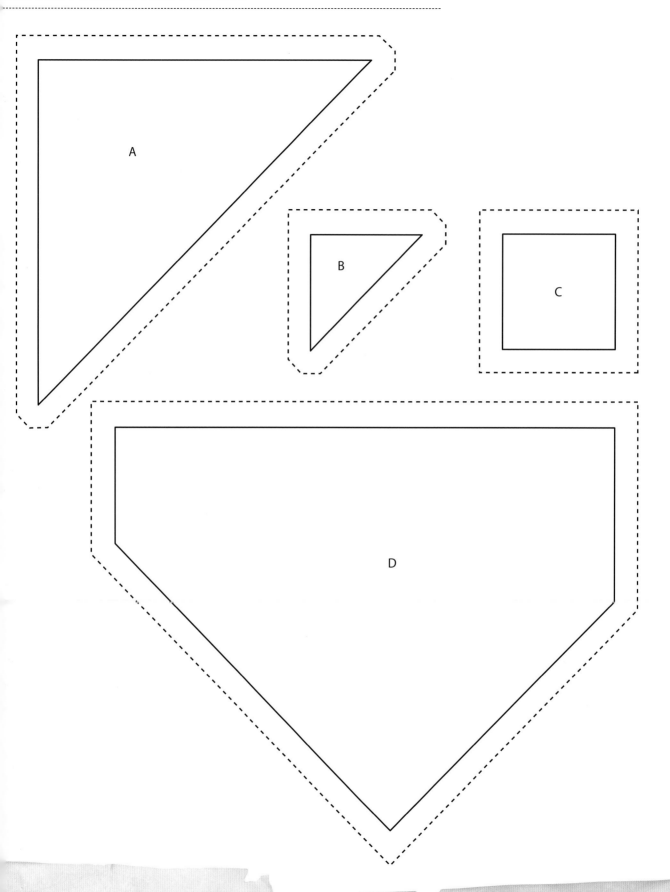

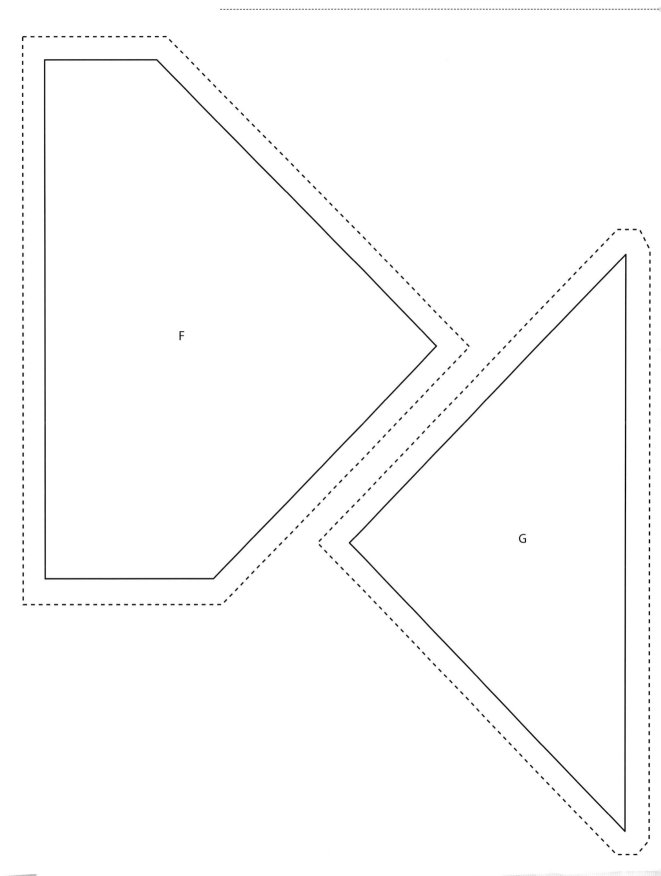

F

G

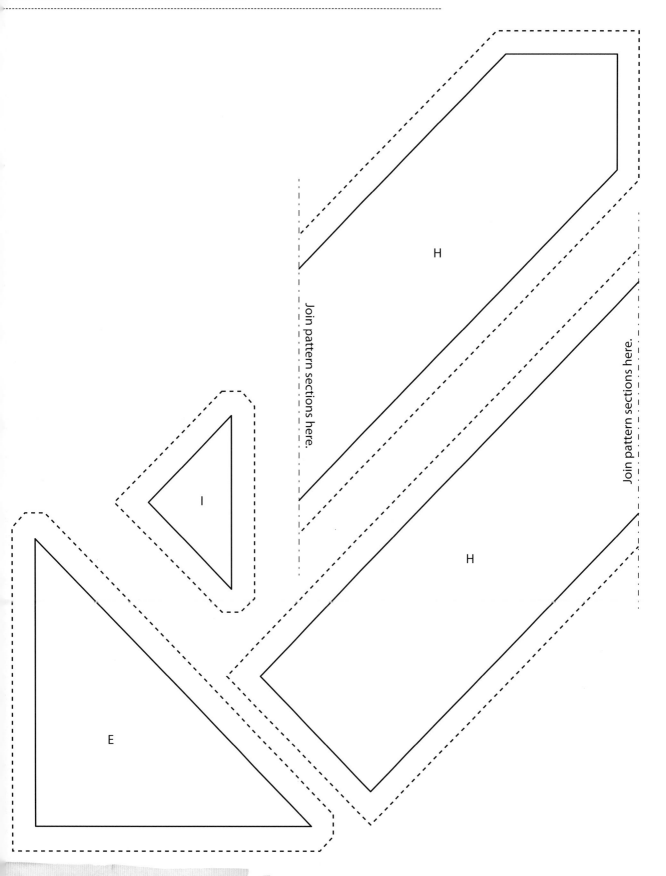

Join pattern sections here.

Join pattern sections here.

H

H

I

E

1928 French Star

Finished block: 12″ × 12″

Fabric Needed

Tan • Medium blue • Dark blue

Cutting Instructions

Use the French Star patterns (pages 21–22).

From tan fabric, cut:

- 4 squares using pattern A
- 4 triangles using pattern B
- 8 ovals using pattern E

From medium blue, cut:

- 4 pieces using pattern D

From dark blue, cut:

- 8 triangles using pattern C

Newspaper Archive

Appeared in *The Kansas City Star* on October 3, 1928 (block #3)

No collection of quilt block designs is complete without one in a star motif. With the pioneer mothers who so ingeniously planned and pieced their own quilts, this symbol was a favorite. The French Star is a Canadian pattern varying the eight-pointed star of diamond-shaped blocks by introducing small melon-shaped pieces of the background color or of contrasting hue. These melon-shaped pieces in turn form a wreath and may divide the star into 2 colors, as rose and pink, 2 shades of green or orange and yellow, as suggested. Make the patterns of cardboard of exactly the same size they are sketched. Then lay the cardboard patterns on the cloth, and trace around with a pencil. These patterns do not allow for a seam, so when you cut them out of the cloth cut the cloth larger to make a seam of the width desired and then sew back to the pencil line. In making the French Star, sew 2 of the cone-shaped pieces to each white triangle, and then sew the corner squares to 2 of these blocks. The small melon-shaped blocks piece onto the center blocks; these in turn sew into a circle to which are added to oblong blocks and strips which were made first. This takes precise piecing, but it makes an usually attractive design when complete, either for patchwork pillows or for a quilt top. For the quilt, piece the star blocks together, using alternate squares of white of exactly the same size as the pieced blocks, and finish with a border of white or color as desired.

To Make the Block

1. Sew the tan ovals (piece E) to the medium blue D pieces.

2. Sew the center of the block together.

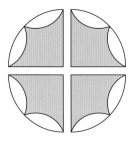

3. Sew a dark blue C triangle to either side of a tan B triangle. Make 4 of these units.

4. Sew the C-B-C units to the center of the block.

5. Inset the 4 corner A squares to complete the block.

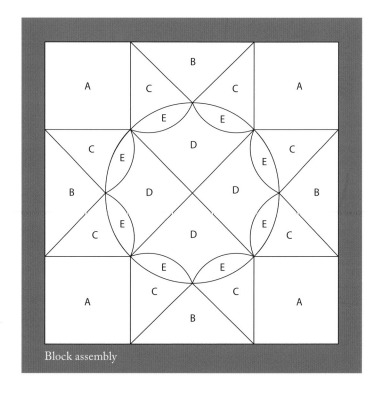

Block assembly

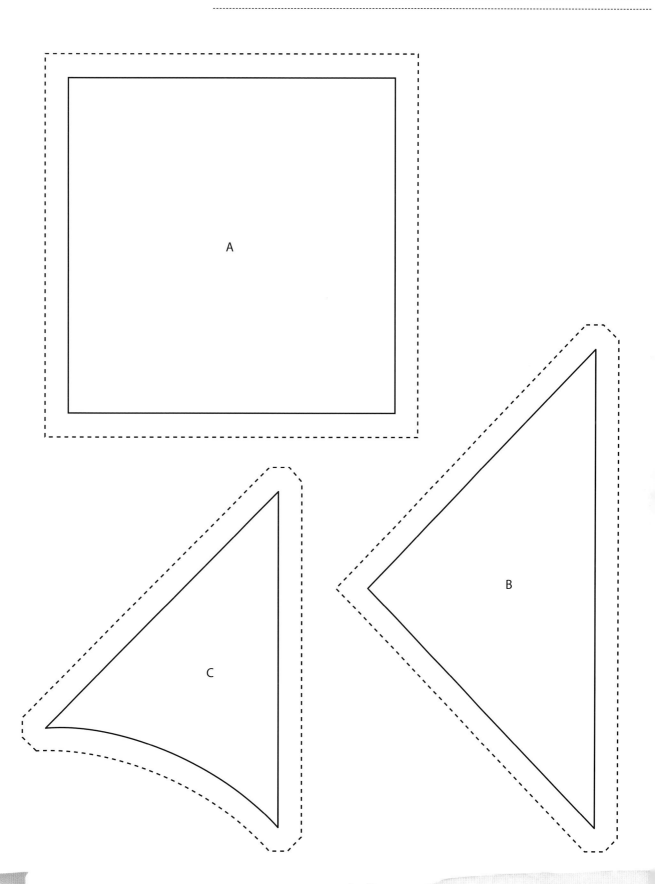

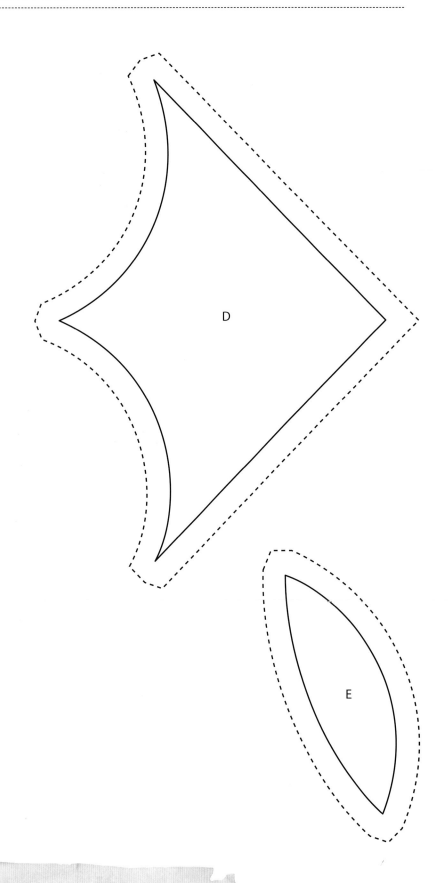

1928 Rob Peter and Pay Paul

Finished block: 12″ × 12″

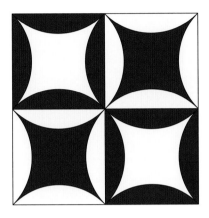

Fabric Needed

Brown plaid • Cream shirting

Cutting Instructions

Use the Rob Peter and Pay Paul patterns (page 25).

From brown plaid fabric, cut:

• 2 pieces using pattern B

• 8 pieces using pattern A

From the shirting, cut:

• 2 pieces using pattern B

• 8 pieces using pattern A

Newspaper Archive

Appeared in *The Kansas City Star* on October 17, 1928 (block #5)

Original size: 5½″. This quilt gets its name from the appearance of the light blocks being cut out to add to the dark, while the dark blocks are trimmed to piece out the light blocks. This procedure is not exactly the case, however, as in reality the blocks must be larger to provide for a seam. Make a cardboard cutting pattern from the sketch given. This pattern does not allow for seams, so draw on the cloth around the cardboard but cut a seam larger and then sew to the pencil line. Rob Peter and Pay Paul looks like a series of circles when set together, but the unit block is square. Of course, half the blocks are made with dark centers and half with light centers surrounded by the darker color. Blue and buff are suggested, but any 2 harmonizing colors make up attractively in this charming old-fashioned design. Patterns of both the center block and parts of the circle are given in the cut in correct size.

To Make the Block

1. Sew the brown plaid A pieces to the shirting B pieces. Make 2.

2. Sew the shirting A pieces to the brown plaid B pieces. Make 2.

3. Sew the 4 units together to complete the block.

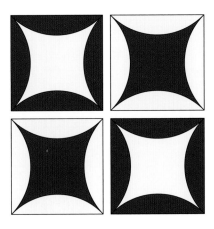

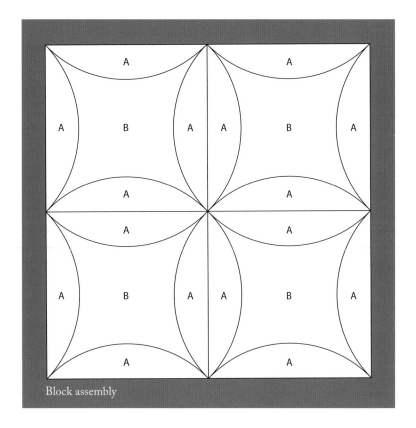

Block assembly

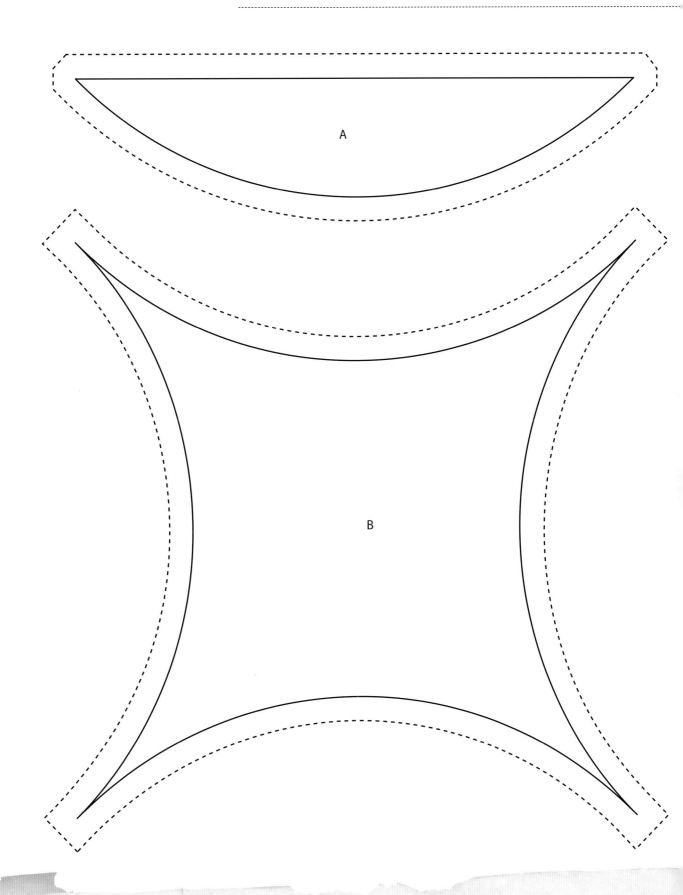

1929 Aircraft Quilt

Finished block: 12″ × 12″

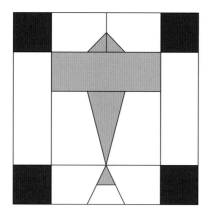

Fabric Needed

Gray • Light blue • Dark blue

Cutting Instructions

Use the Aircraft Quilt patterns (pages 29–31).

From gray fabric, cut:

• 1 rectangle using pattern D

• 1 triangle using pattern I

• 2 triangles using pattern K

• 1 triangle using pattern L

From light blue fabric, cut:

• 2 rectangles using pattern D
• 1 piece using pattern B
• 1 piece using pattern C
• 1 piece using pattern H

• 1 piece using pattern J
• 1 piece using pattern G
• 1 piece using pattern E
• 1 piece using pattern F

From dark blue fabric, cut:

• 4 squares using pattern A

Newspaper Archive

Appeared in *The Kansas City Star* on July 13, 1929 (block #43)

Here is modern design in pieced quilts. Mrs. Otto Prell of Miami, Oklahoma, sent *The Star* this design just as 2 transcontinental airplane lines are being inaugurated in their flight through Kansas City from coast to coast. May it have its place in the history of the world as emblematic of this age, just as our great-grandmothers designed the saw-tooth and the churn dash and the Log Cabin patterns which were symbolic of the times in which they lived. Thank you, Mrs. Prell; we are delighted to see this modern motif in quilt blocks. This quilt may be set together in several interesting ways; one is to arrange the planes in V-formation, alternating them with plain blocks or in 2 V-formations, one right behind the other, the first plane of the last V just back of the first V. Or the planes may be alternated with plain blocks over the quilt. Dark blue planes set together with a light blue is a suggestion. These single blocks make very nice cushions.

To Make the Block

1. Sew a gray K triangle to the light blue B piece and one to the light blue C piece.

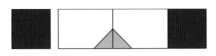

2. Sew the 2 pieces together then stitch a dark blue square to either end.

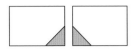

3. Sew the light blue H piece to the gray I piece. Add the light blue J piece.

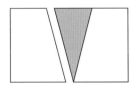

4. Stitch the gray D rectangle to the top.

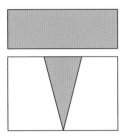

5. Now sew a light blue D rectangle to either side.

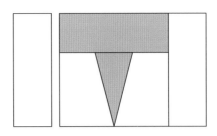

6. Sew the light blue F piece to the gray L triangle.

7. Now sew the light blue G piece to one side of the triangles and the light blue E piece to the other.

8. Add a dark blue A square to each end.

9. You now have 3 rows. Sew the rows together to complete the block.

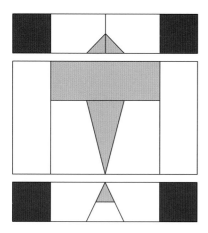

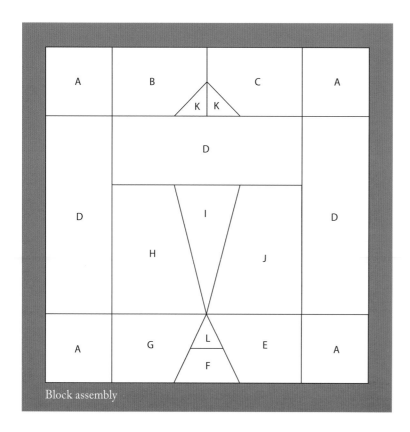

Block assembly

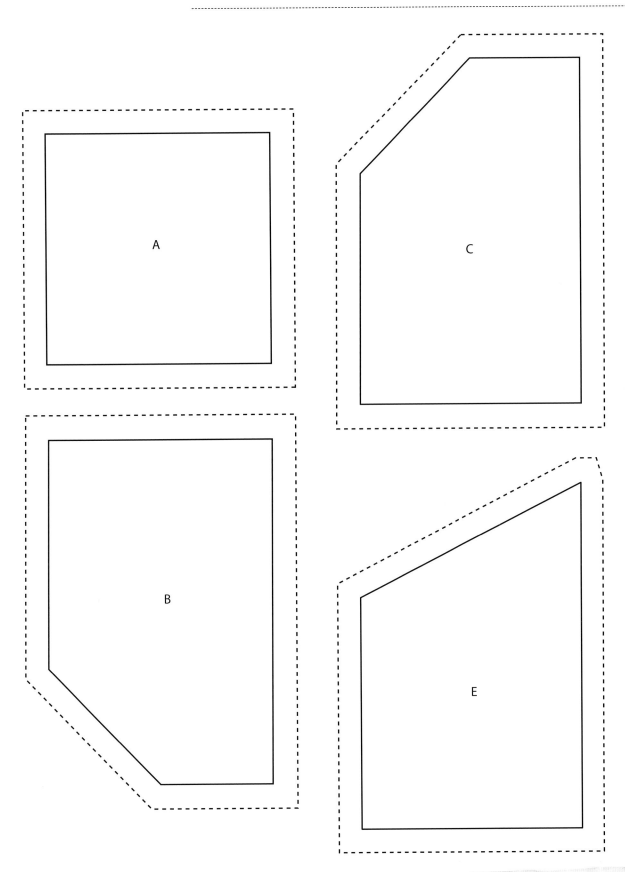

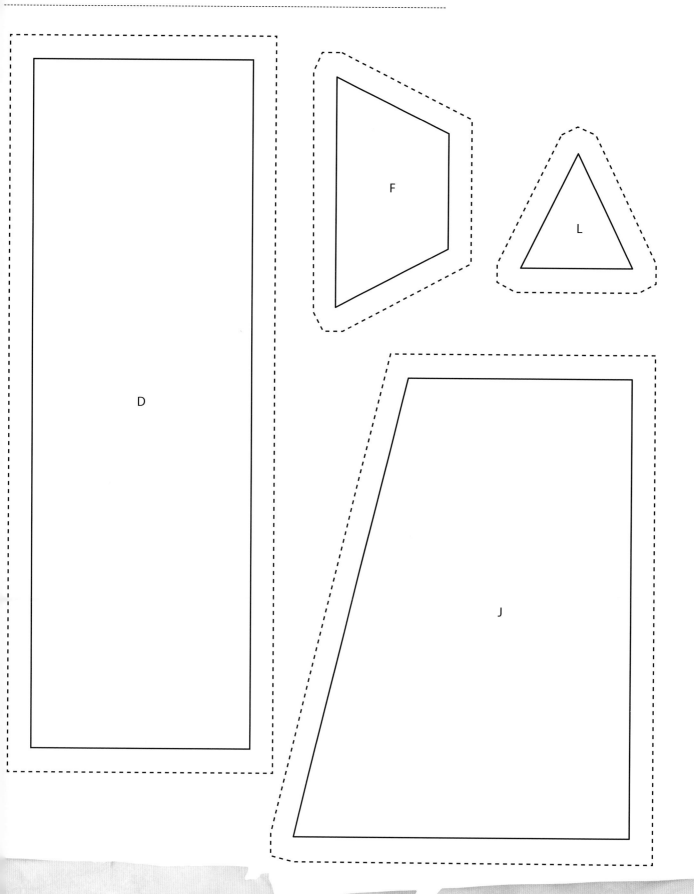

D

F

L

J

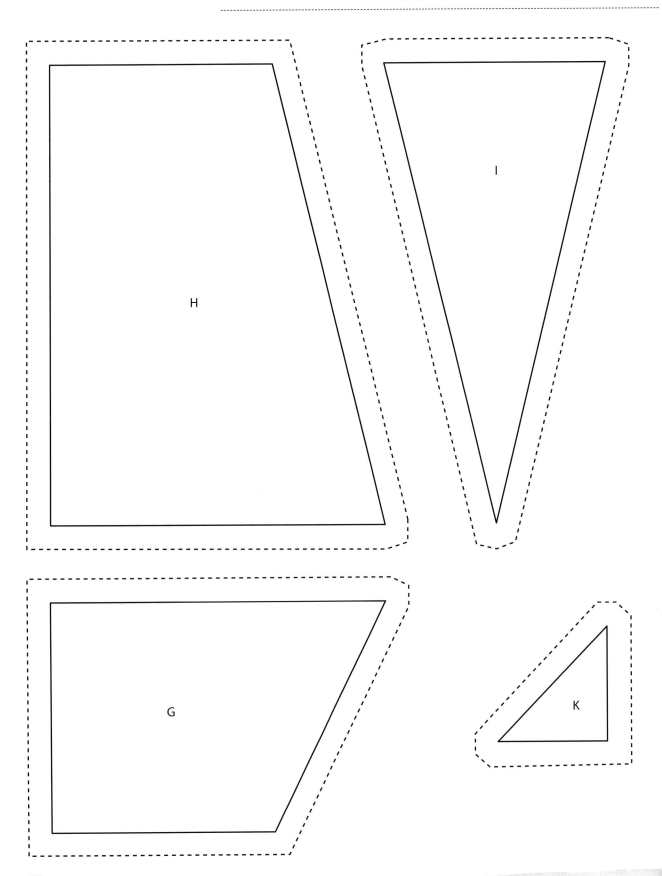

H

I

G

K

1929 Beautiful Star

Finished block: 12″ × 12″

Fabric Needed

Light blue • Dark blue • Yellow

Cutting Instructions

Use the Beautiful Star patterns (pages 34–35).

From light blue fabric, cut:

• 4 pieces using pattern A

From dark blue fabric, cut:

• 4 triangles using pattern C

From yellow fabric, cut:

• 4 diamonds using pattern B

Newspaper Archive

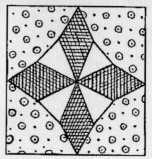

Appeared in *The Kansas City Star* on March 16, 1929 (block #26)

Variety is unlimited in the field of quilt patterns. That is one secret of their fascination which continues from generation to generation. The beautiful star design is pieced of chintz or calico, which makes part of the block and sets all blocks together. The block itself is 10″ square. When a yellow oil print combines with dull red and unbleached muslin in the blocks, it makes a coverlet well worth making. Or the "star" may be made in a pale green plain material and set on a background of green print.

To Make the Block

1. Sew a dark blue C triangle to a yellow diamond. Make 4.

2. Sew the units together.

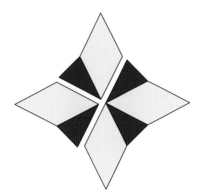

3. Add the light blue A units to complete the block.

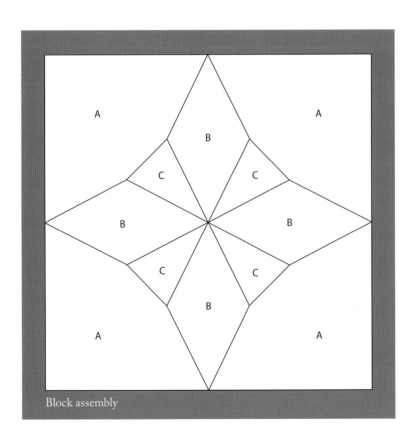

Block assembly

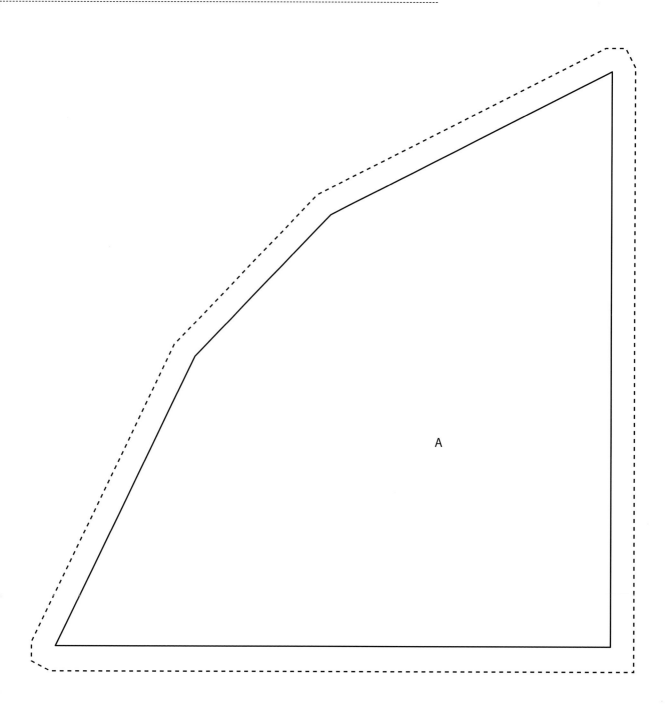

A

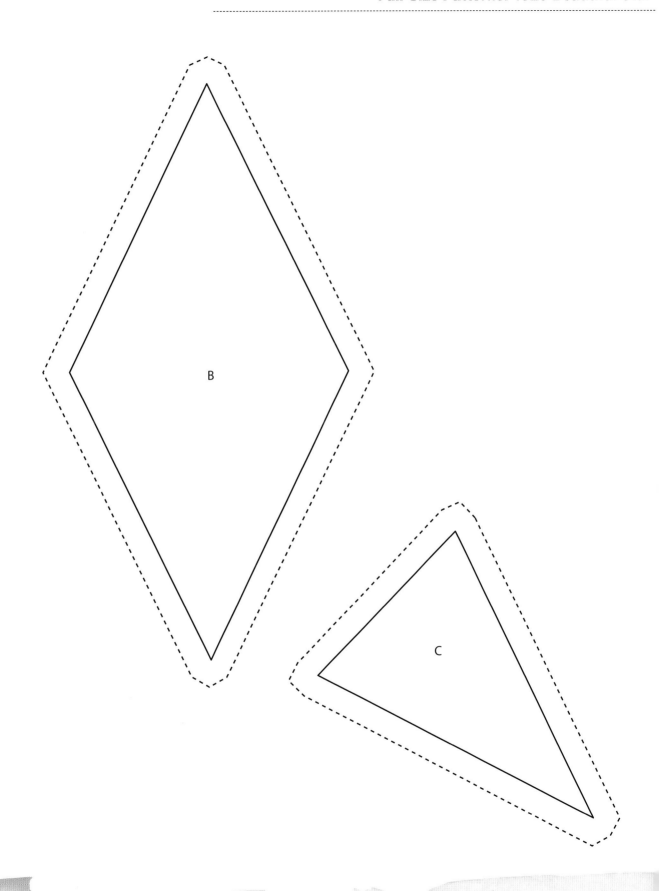

B

C

1929 Double Nine-Patch

Finished block: 9″ × 9″

Fabric Needed

Dark • Light

Cutting Instructions

Use the Double Nine-Patch patterns (page 38). This block can also be made using a rotary cutter and ruler.

From dark fabric, cut:

• 4 squares 3½″ × 3½″ (pattern A)

• 5 squares 1½″ × 1½″ (pattern B)

From light fabric, cut:

• 4 squares 3½″ × 3½″ (pattern A)

• 4 squares 1½″ × 1½″ (pattern B)

To Make the Block

1. Sew the dark and light 1½″ squares together in rows of 3, alternating the colors. Sew the 3 rows together. This makes up the center square of the block.

2. Sew a dark 3½″ square to either side of a light 3½″ square. Make 2 strips.

3. Sew a light 3½″ square to either side of the center square.

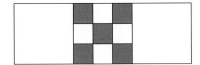

4. Sew the 3 rows together to complete the block.

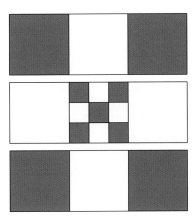

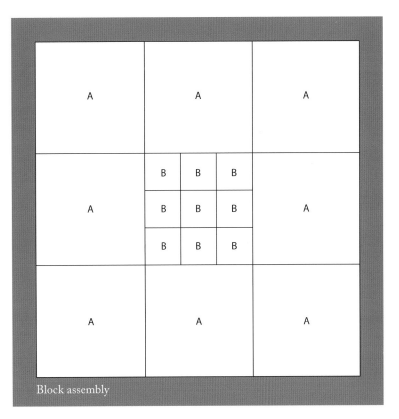

Block assembly

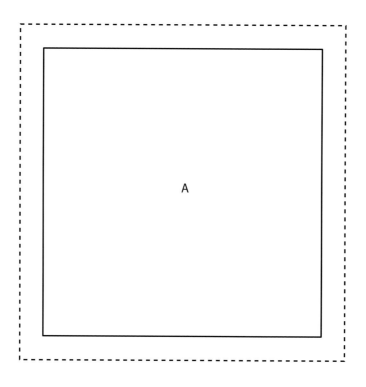

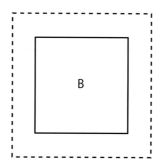

1930s

See the
Turkey
Tracks block
(page 114).

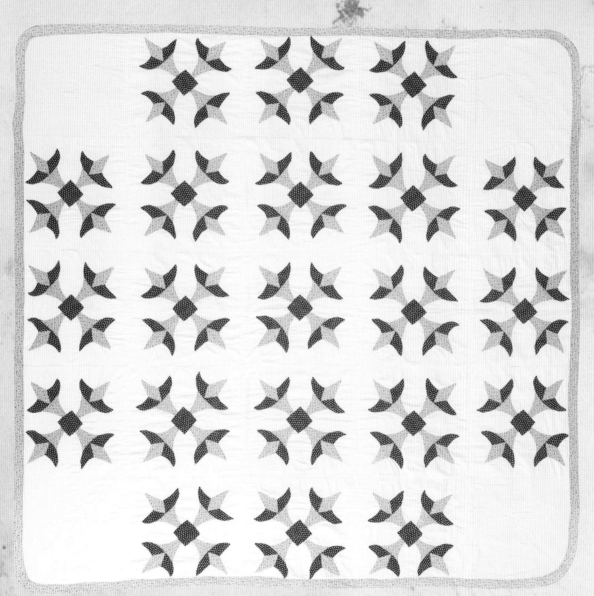

Turkey Tracks, owned by Wendy Dilllingham; quilted by Mayme Julia Jacobson Smith, circa 1940–1950

Eveline Foland

Mystery Designer

by Barbara Brackman

Eveline Foland's graceful drawings appeared in *The Kansas City Star* over her bold signature from March 1929 through 1932. At first, Foland's quilt patterns alternated with designs by Ruby McKim (page 10), but soon Foland conducted the column on her own, drawing about 130 designs. Most were her illustrations of traditional quilts shared by readers. She also designed several of her own modern patterns, inspired by contemporary taste. The flower in "Eveline's Posey" (that's the way she spelled *posey*) reflects both the simple shapes of modernism and the graceful lines of art nouveau, characteristics of her distinctive style.

Eveline Alice Smith was born January 22, 1893, in Kansas City, daughter of Canadians Elliot F. and Lily L. Whitelaw Smith. Quilt pattern historian Wilene Smith has found much about Eveline's early life and published information in the (Kansas) *Baldwin Ledger* February 28, 1985. Eveline was the youngest of three children. She graduated from Kansas City's Central High School in 1908 and spent a year at the Kansas City Art Institute in 1910. Eveline (pattern collectors pronounce her name *eh-vah-LEEN*) taught at the Jane Hayes Gates School, later incorporated into Manual High School. The school offered courses for women over fourteen years of age, teaching them the trades of dressmaking, millinery, factory sewing, and commercial art.

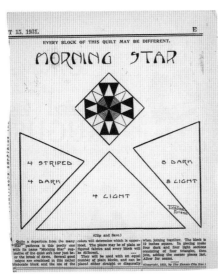

"Morning Star" with Foland's high-style lettering appeared in August 1931.

She married a salesman, James E. Foland, in 1922, and they adopted a boy, James Elliot Foland, about 1925. She began illustrating *Star* fashion and home decoration features about the same time. She and Foland divorced in 1931. Quilt historians lose track of Eveline Foland in 1933 after her last pattern appeared in *The Kansas City Star*. For a while, she continued freelance fashion illustration in Kansas City. She probably remarried, changed her name, and moved from the area, making her difficult to find in public records, especially during the Depression when city directories and phone books were rather sparse. Her later life remains a mystery.

Edna Marie Dunn
The Star's Fashion Illustrator

by Barbara Brackman

In 1932, a new signature appeared in *The Kansas City Star*'s quilt pattern column. *The Star*'s fashion illustrator, Edna Marie Dunn, took over the column after Eveline Foland's departure. Dunn signed only four of her early patterns, but she was the feature's anonymous editor for the next three decades. Between 1932 and 1961, Dunn edited and drew the hundreds of quilt patterns printed in *The Star*.

Dunn asked readers throughout the subscription area to send in favorite designs. Each week she drafted the patterns with her T-square and ruler, printing the suggested name and crediting the contributor. If the pattern was unnamed, Dunn did some quick research to find a name or made one up herself. She told Louise Townsend, who interviewed her in 1978, that "she was too busy with her fashion illustration work to spend much time researching quilt names or designing patterns."

Over the years, her quilt illustrations seem to reflect the time she had to devote to the drawing. The earlier designs have some of the flair that McKim and Foland added to the feature, but as the decades went by, style and space were minimal.

Edna Marie Dunn (1893–1983) was born in Chicago and moved to Kansas City as a child. She graduated from Christian College in Columbia, Missouri, and attended the Chicago Academy of Art. She returned to Kansas City, illustrating fashion for department stores such as Harzfeld's, Woolf Brothers, and Rothschild's. In 1922, Dunn won a competition to become a fashion artist for *The Kansas City Star*.

Edna Marie Dunn taught many of Kansas City's aspiring artists at her own school at 3820 Main Street, the Edna Marie Dunn School of Fashion, which she began in 1938. She and her husband Frank E. Douglass also operated a stationery business that published cards and gift books in Edna's designs. When Frank died in 1964, she retired. Edna lived to be 90.

Needlecraft Service and Home Art Studios

by Barbara Brackman

Editors at *The Kansas City Star* knew how Depression-era readers loved the quilt pattern features, so they subscribed to two different mail-order patterns. Quilters looked forward to the full-sized Sunday pattern drawn by Edna Marie Dunn. During the week, they read two smaller reader service features: one from New York's Needlecraft Service, the other from a Des Moines company known to pattern collectors as Home Art Studios. These smaller columns advertised patterns that could be ordered through the mail. For Needlecraft Service patterns, a drawing of a patchwork quilt and a paragraph of description were followed by a last line reading "Send 10 cents for the pattern to *The Kansas City Star*, Needlecraft Dept., Kansas City, Mo."

Continued on next page.

Continued from page 43.

The Star forwarded orders to a pattern source in New York City that went by a number of official names. Quilt pattern collectors know little about this company, which was formed as Needlecraft Service in 1932. The name was changed to Reader Mail in 1944. Over the years, they've offered patterns for all kinds of needlework including crochet and clothing.

Needlecraft's patterns appeared in dozens of newspapers in the 1930s. The column ran under the names Laura Wheeler or Alice Brooks, fictional authors who gave a personal touch to the feature. *The Star* patterns printed before World War II used no byline, so pattern collectors have learned to recognize the Needlecraft Service designs by their distinctive drawing style, which featured detailed calicoes in blocks drawn side by side to emphasize complex secondary designs. Many readers were inspired by the lovely drawings and the innovative designs to invest their dime in "stamps or coin, coin preferred."

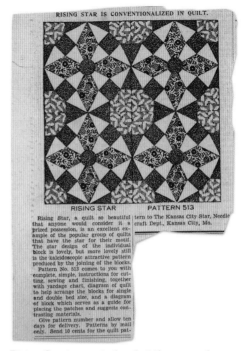

Rising Star is a typical early 30's pattern from the Needlecraft Service Company, highlighting original design with sophisticated secondary patterning. In some newspapers, the feature appeared under the signature Laura Wheeler, but the early *Star* patterns were anonymous.

These patterns were neither feature nor advertisement, but something called a "reader service feature." Newspapers subscribed to the feature, knowing that readers, especially rural readers, enjoyed the opportunity to order fashion and crafts by mail. The paper and the pattern company shared those many dimes.

The Needlecraft Service's New York addresses, which varied over the years, were in the neighborhood served by the Old Chelsea Station post office. Before the era of postal zones and zip codes, the words "Old Chelsea Station, New York City," were enough to direct the dime and the pattern request to the correct address.

Replies came by mail in an envelope with the return address of the local newspaper or the New York office. Pattern sheets inside were as sophisticated as the drawing in the ads, including a good deal of information on about 15″ × 20″ of tissue or newsprint.

Quilt historian Wilene Smith has determined that Nathan Kogan, Max Levine, and Anne Borne formed a business called Needlecraft Service, Inc., in 1932. As yet, pattern historians know nothing about the actual designers who created the innovative patterns and drawings. To add to confusion about company history, Smith found that Needlecraft Service set up two competing branches to make the most of cities with competing newspapers. Laura Wheeler might offer patterns in one paper, Alice Brooks in another. Each "designer" had a different New York City address, which Smith thinks were mail drops, to distinguish the bylines. The company also used regional names, such as Carol Curtis in the Midwest and Mary Cullen in the northwest.

Like the Laura Wheeler feature, Home Art Studios sent *The Star* a weekly advertisement featuring a drawing of a quilt with information about the design and instructions to send a dime or a quarter to "Pattern Department," in care of *The Star*. *The Star* forwarded the orders to Des Moines. Again, the columns were anonymous in Kansas City, although some newspapers used the byline "Bettina."

Bettina was the pen name of a man. Hubert Ver Mehren (1892–1972) had inherited a mail-order notions company from his father, a company that had two branches: the ideal Button and Pleating Company, in Omaha, Nebraska, where Hubert grew up, and the Iowa Button and Pleating Company in Des Moines, the branch Hubert managed after his World War I service and 1920 marriage. They sold notions, such as braid and beads, through mail-order catalogs and did pleating, scalloping, buttonholes, and hem-stitching to order. The companies also stamped cloth with patterns for needlework corset covers, collars, tablecloths, and pillowcases.

As colorfast cotton embroidery floss in a variety of shades became widely available, Hubert realized there was a market for stamped quilt blocks to be embroidered. He also realized he could stamp fabric for geometric patchwork, making kits for pieced designs. With his wife, Mary Jacobs, he ran a thriving quilt pattern business between 1931 and 1934.

Ver Mehren was quite a draftsman. His stamped kits for complex stars and sunbursts that covered the whole quilt top became a trademark. The medallions offered a real challenge to skilled seamstresses, who must have been pleased with his accuracy. The bread and butter of Home Art's business, however, was the stamped blocks, pillowcases, and dresser scarves that appealed to the average seamstress. Although the company's heyday was short (Mary became ill and Hubert devoted time to caring for her and then raising their children after her death), Home Art Studios strongly influenced the look of mid-twentieth-century quilts.

1930 Mexican Star

Finished block: 12″ × 12″

Fabric Needed

Tan • Medium purple • Dark purple

Cutting Instructions

Use the Mexican Star patterns (pages 48–49). This block can also be made using a rotary cutter and ruler for the measured pieces.

From tan fabric, cut:

• 1 square 7¼″ × 7¼″. Cut the square from corner to corner twice on the diagonal or cut 4 triangles using pattern C.

• 5 squares 1¹⁵⁄₁₆″ × 1¹⁵⁄₁₆″ (pattern F)

• 4 squares 2⅞″ × 2⅞″. Cut each square from corner to corner once on the diagonal or cut 8 triangles using pattern B.

From medium purple, cut:

• 4 pieces using pattern D

• 4 pieces using pattern E

From dark purple, cut:

• 4 squares 1¹⁵⁄₁₆″ × 1¹⁵⁄₁₆″ (pattern F)

• 4 pieces using pattern A

Newspaper Archive

Appeared in *The Kansas City Star* on July 5, 1930 (block #104) and December 31, 1941 (block #672)

From 1930: Recently a quilt collector found a beautiful old Mexican Star quilt up in the mountains of York state. It was a handsome specimen in red and blues. How these same lovely patterns are found north, south, east, and west testify of the far-flung ties that bound together the scattered settlers of Mexican War days, when this pattern was doubtless originated. This is rather an intricate pattern to piece, but the effect when set together entirely of pieced blocks looks more beautiful than bewildering. If you are a quilt enthusiast, Mexican Star will tempt you. Seams are not allowed.

From 1941: From her collection of quilt block designs, Mrs. Melvin Nielsen of Boone, Colorado, has lent the Mexican Star, a popular pattern, which was printed in *The Weekly Star* several years ago.

To Make the Block

You will sew this block together on the diagonal.

1. Sew the B triangles to the D and E pieces.

2. Sew the F squares together to make a nine-patch unit for the center of the block.

3. To make the upper right part of the block, sew a C triangle to the D and E pieces.

4. To complete the upper right part of the block, sew an A strip between the 2 triangles made in Step 3.

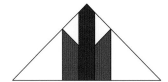

5. Next make the center portion of the block. Sew the remaining B-D and B-E units to the A strips. You should have 2 units. Sew the 2 units to the center nine-patch.

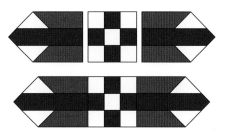

6. Sew the 3 rows together to complete the block.

Block assembly

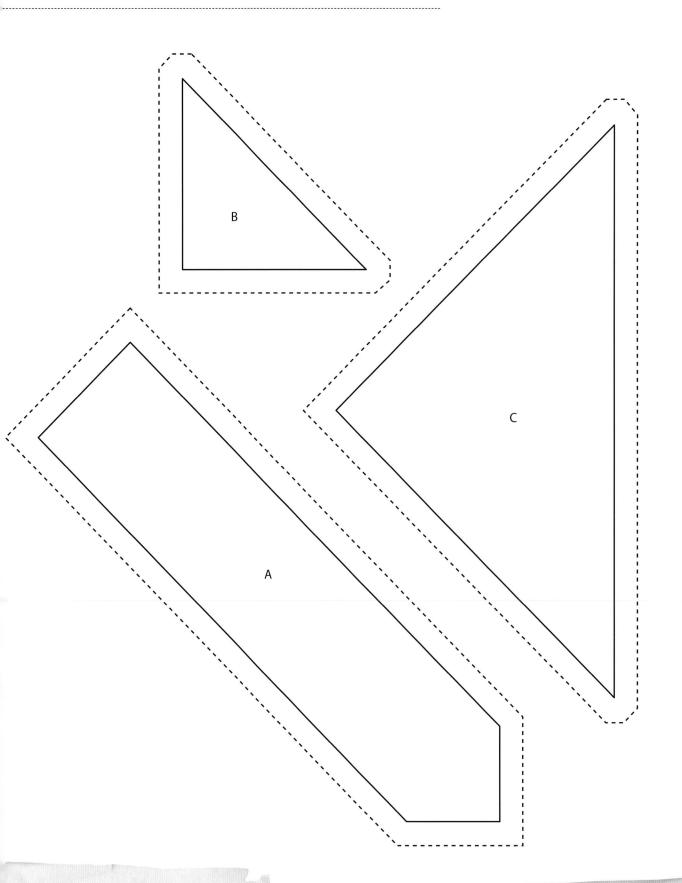

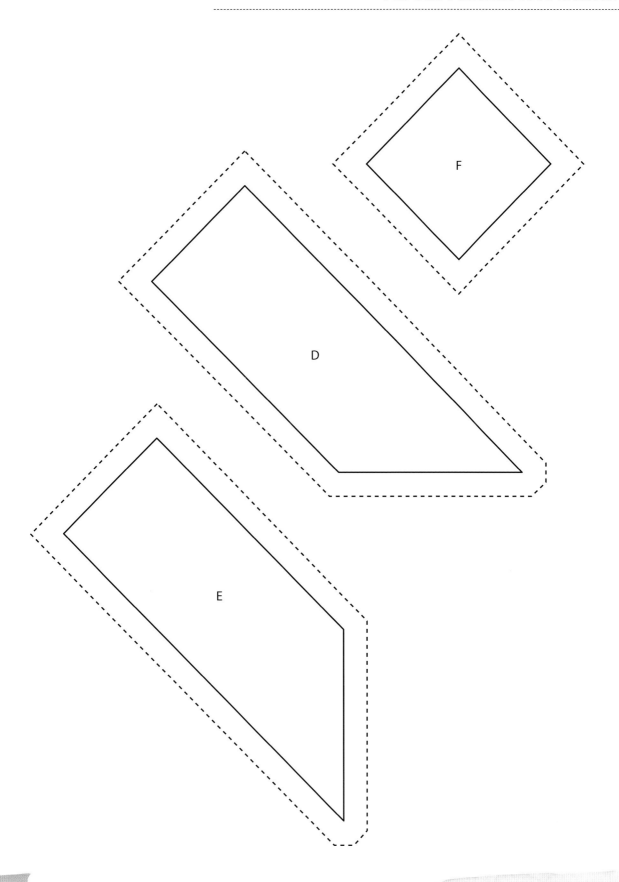

1930 Blazing Star

Finished block: 12″ × 12″

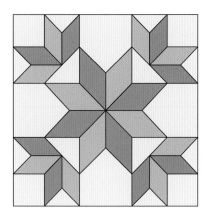

Fabric Needed

Double pink print • Green print • Light tan

Cutting Instructions

Use the Blazing Star patterns (pages 53–55).
This block can also be made using a rotary
cutter and ruler for the measured piece.

From light tan, cut:

• 4 squares 2½″ × 2½″ (pattern A)

• 8 triangles using pattern B

• 4 pieces using pattern C

• 4 triangles using pattern G

From double pink print, cut:

• 8 diamonds using pattern F

• 4 diamonds using pattern E

Newspaper Archive

Appeared in *The Kansas City Star*
on February 15, 1930 (block #84)

The Blazing Star is an extremely interesting block in 3 colors. If one cared to
carry out this idea, red, yellow, and white
would be the most effective. However,
the block would be beautiful in a combination of solid colors and a figured
background of 3 pastel colors: pink, blue,
and a lavender background, for example.
In piecing this block it would be well
to do the 4 corners first, then the white
patches between these squares, joining
the 2 diamond-shaped patches at the top.
The rest is a simple matter. This block,
when complete, is 13½″ square. Seams
are not allowed on these patterns.

From green print, cut:

• 8 diamonds using pattern H

• 4 diamonds using pattern D

To Make the Block

1. Stitch the E and D diamonds together into pairs. These will be inset seams.

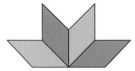

2. Sew the pairs together to make 2 halves of the center star. These will be inset seams.

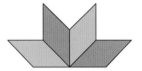

3. Sew the 2 halves together. These will be inset seams.

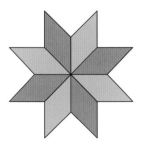

4. Make a corner unit by sewing the H and F diamonds into pairs. Sew 2 pairs together. These will be inset seams.

5. Add the G triangle and inset the B triangles and an A square. Make 4 of these corner units.

6. Inset a C piece between 2 star points. Then inset 2 corner units.

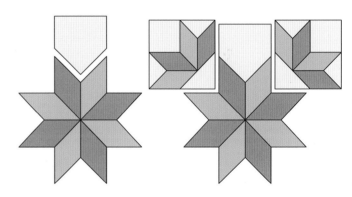

7. Now inset a C piece under each corner unit.

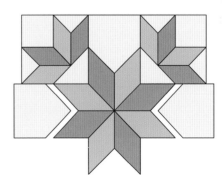

8. Add the 2 remaining corner units.

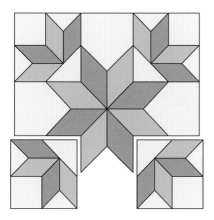

9. Inset the last C piece to complete the block.

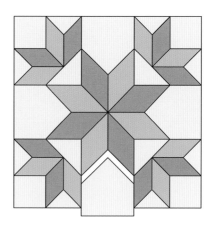

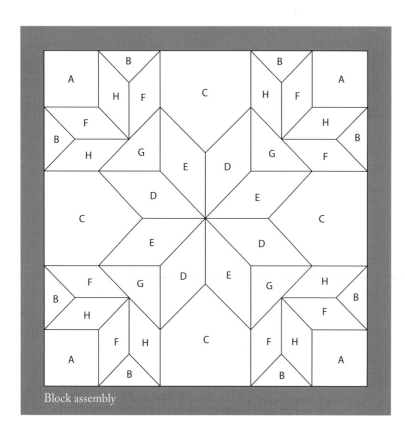

Block assembly

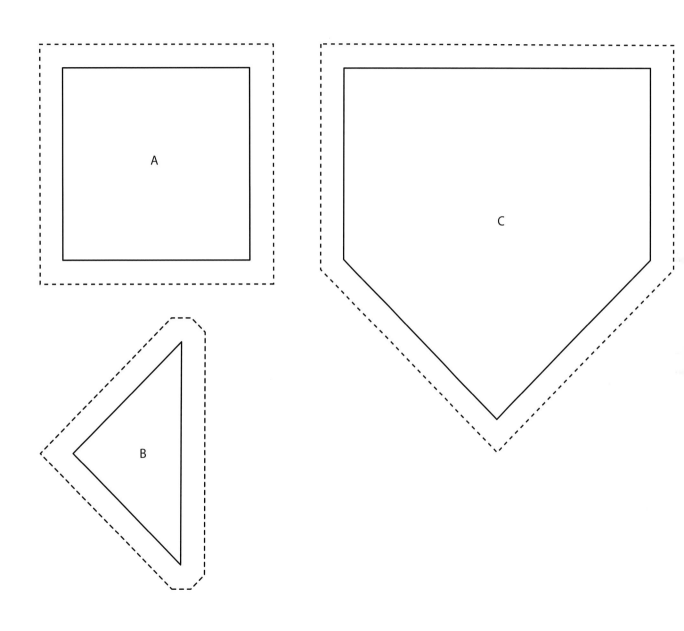

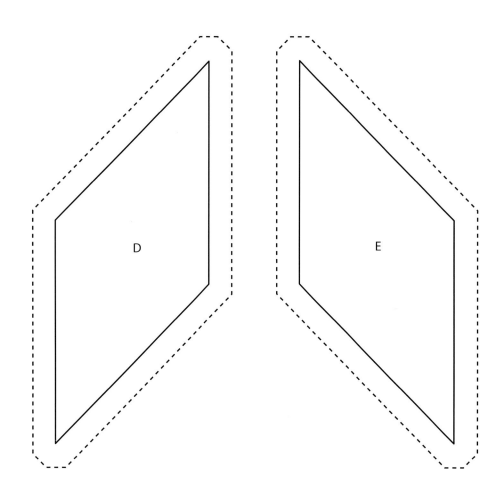

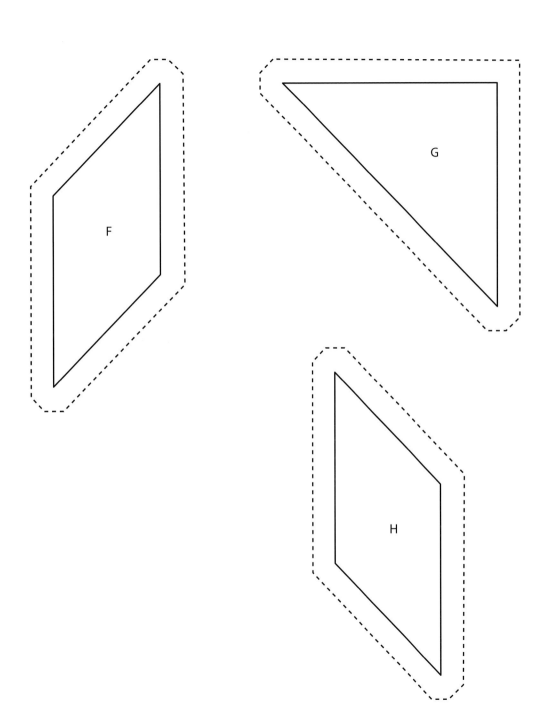

1930 Grape Basket

Finished block: 11⅞″ × 11⅞″

Fabric Needed

Cream • Light purple • Dark purple
Light green • Dark green

Cutting Instructions

Use the Grape Basket patterns (pages 59–60). This block can also be made using a rotary cutter and ruler for the measured piece.

From cream fabric, cut:

- 1 square 2⅞″ × 2⅞″ (pattern A)

- 2 rectangles using pattern D

- 1 triangle using pattern E

- 2 triangles using pattern C

- 5 triangles using pattern B

From light purple fabric, cut:

- 6 triangles using pattern B

- 1 triangle using pattern E

From dark purple fabric, cut:

- 4 triangles using pattern B

From the light green fabric, cut:

- 3 triangles using pattern B

From dark green fabric, cut:

- 1 triangle using pattern E

- 2 triangles using pattern B

Newspaper Archive

Appeared in *The Kansas City Star* on March 8, 1930 (block #87)

Basket quilts are always popular. Here are several charming versions easy to piece. The main part of this one is a four-patch of pieced squares as indicated by the extended lines. To this the long strips with a small triangle on the ends are added, then the final bottom triangle to complete. The grape basket completes into a block 10″ square if seams are added to the unit patterns here given. It should be set together on the diagonal with alternate plain squares and half-squares of white to the edges. The 25 blocks plus a 6″ border and binding makes a full-sized quilt.

To Make the Block

1. Make 2 Flying Geese units by sewing a light purple B triangle and a dark purple B triangle to the 2 cream-colored C triangles.

2. Make half-square triangle units by sewing the following triangles together.

• 2 half-square triangles using cream and light purple

• 2 half-square triangles using light and dark purple

• 3 half-square triangles using light green and cream

4. You'll also need to make 1 half-square triangle using the light purple and the dark green E triangles.

5. Sew the top row of the basket together. You should have a square, a half- square triangle, and a Flying Geese unit.

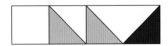

6. The second row is made up of half-square triangles sewn together.

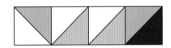

7. Now sew the remaining Flying Geese unit to 2 half-square triangles. Add these to the large purple and green half-square triangle.

8. Sew the rows you have made so far together.

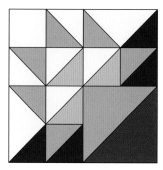

9. Sew the green B triangles to the cream rectangles. Sew one to each side of the basket.

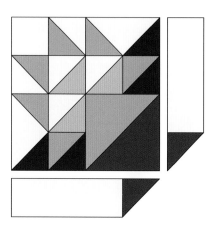

10. Sew the remaining cream triangle to the base of the basket to complete the block.

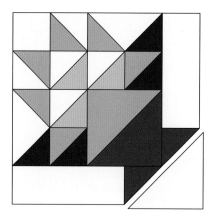

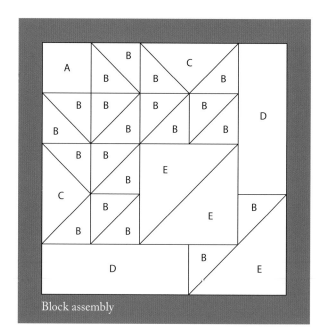

Block assembly

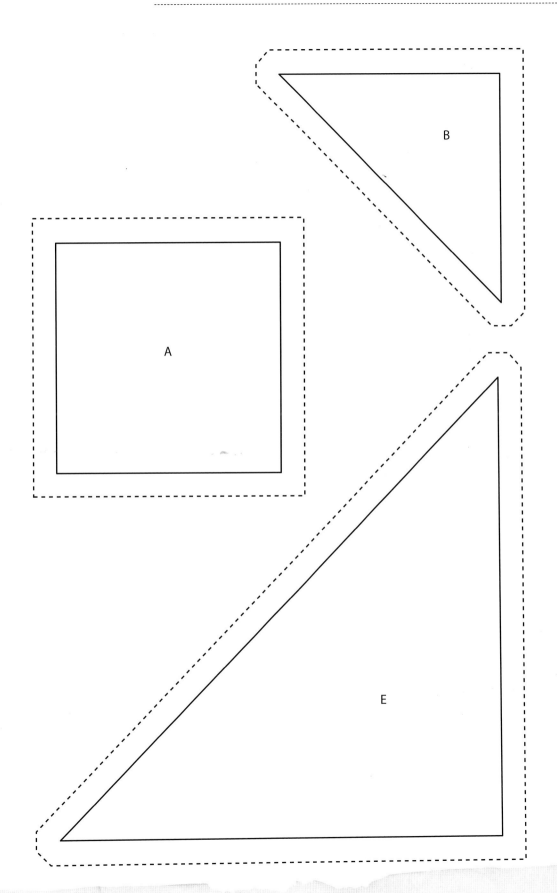

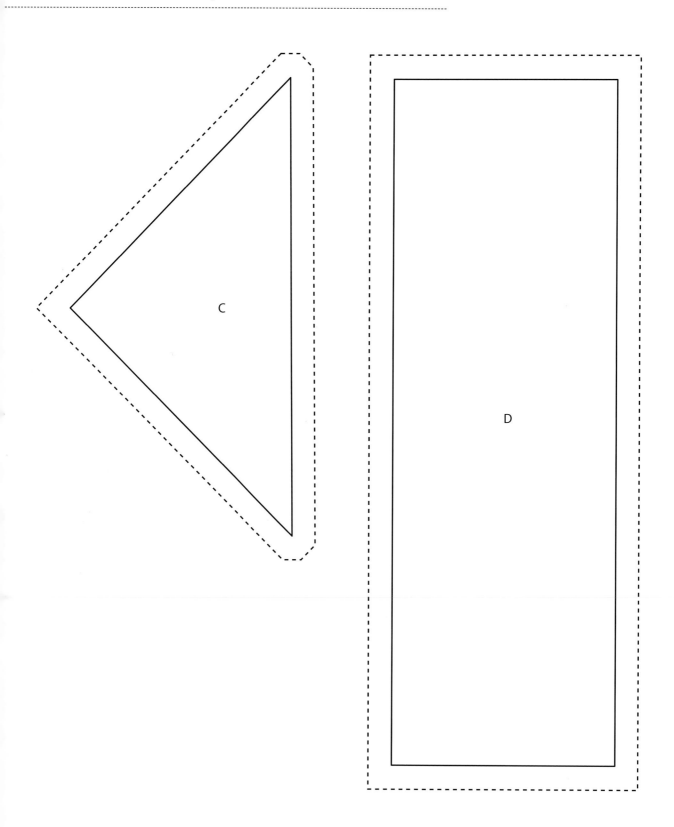

1930 Corn and Beans

Finished block: 12″ × 12″

Fabric Needed

Cream • Green • Yellow

Cutting Instructions

Use the Corn and Beans patterns (page 64). This block can also be made using a rotary cutter and ruler.

From cream-colored fabric, cut:

- 3 squares 4⅞″ × 4⅞″. Cut each square from corner to corner once on the diagonal to make 6 triangles or use pattern A.

- 10 squares 2⅞″ × 2⅞″. Cut each square from corner to corner once on the diagonal to make 20 triangles or use pattern B.

Newspaper Archive

Appeared in *The Kansas City Star* on January 11, 1930 (block #79)

Original size: 12″. A variation of the old Shoo-Fly quilt is most originally called the Corn and Beans. It is an effective nine-patch design whose charmingly patterned bits of appliqués make up into a surprisingly pretty quilt. One can easily discern the "corn" by its triangular shape and the other blocks, which are developed in printed fabric, must be the "beans." Most of the nine-patch designs are of unquestionable colonial origin. Some of the more popular ones are Duck and Ducklings, A Young Man's Fancy, and Philadelphia Pavement.

From green fabric, cut:

- 2 squares 2⅞″ × 2⅞″. Cut each square from corner to corner once on the diagonal to make 4 triangles or use pattern B.

- 1 square 5¼″ × 5¼″. Cut the square from corner to corner twice on the diagonal to make 4 triangles or use pattern C.

From yellow fabric, cut:

- 1 square 4⅞″ × 4⅞″. Cut the square from corner to corner once on the diagonal to make 2 triangles or use pattern A.

- 4 squares 2⅞″ × 2⅞″. Cut each square from corner to corner once on the diagonal to make 8 triangles or use pattern B.

To Make the Block

1. Sew a yellow A triangle to a cream A triangle. Make 2 units and sew them together.

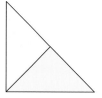 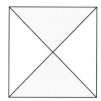

2. Sew a cream B triangle to either side of a green B triangle. Make 4 strips.

3. Sew the 4 strips to the center of the block.

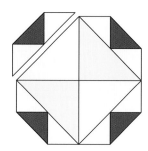

4. Now stitch the green C triangles in place.

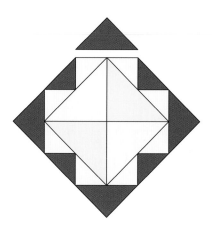

5. Sew 5 B triangles together into a strip, alternating cream and yellow triangles. Begin and end the strip with a cream triangle. Make 4 and add them to the block.

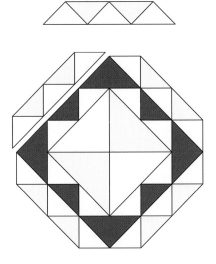

6. Add a cream A triangle to each corner to complete the block.

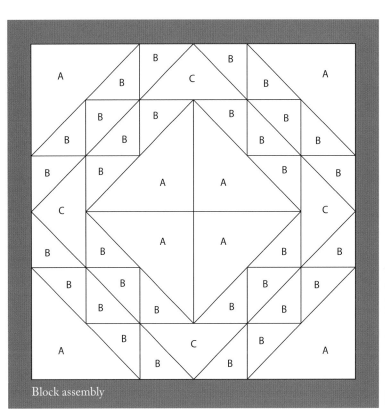

Block assembly

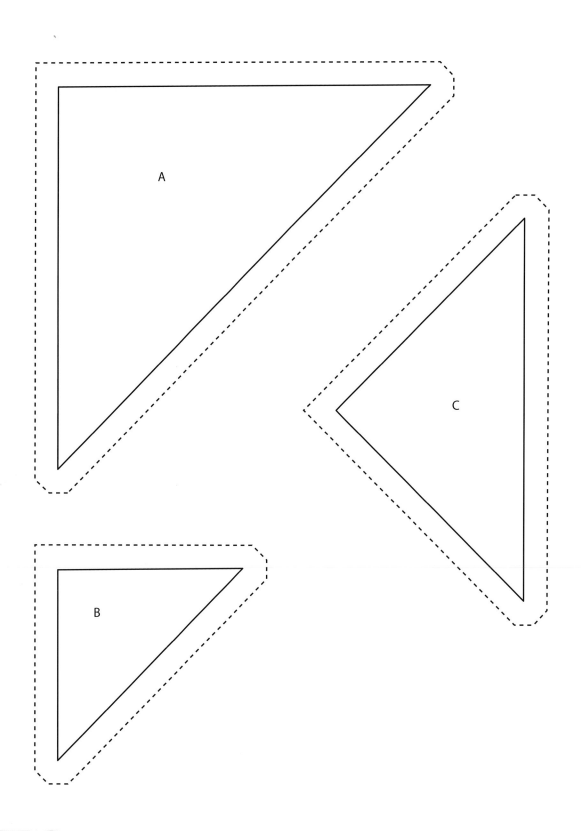

1931 Gold Fish

Finished block: 12″ × 12″

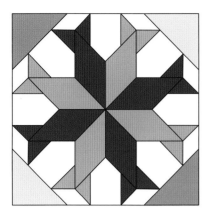

Fabric Needed

Light blue • Medium blue
Gold • Brown • Medium brown

Cutting Instructions

Use the Gold Fish patterns (pages 68–70). This block can also be made using a rotary cutter and ruler for the measured pieces.

From medium brown fabric, cut:

• 1 square 4⅜″ × 4⅜″. Cut the square from corner to corner once on the diagonal or cut 2 triangles using pattern A.

From medium blue fabric, cut:

• 1 square 4⅜″ × 4⅜″. Cut the square from corner to corner once on the diagonal or cut 2 triangles using pattern A.

Newspaper Archive

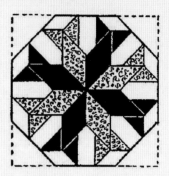

Appeared in *The Kansas City Star* on December 12, 1931 (block #200) and December 10, 1935 (block #396)

Original size: 17″.

From 1931: This old pattern is a modification of the familiar Dove in the Window design. It makes a lovely cushion as well as a quilt. The goldfish are to be in yellow and the surrounding blocks in the pale green of the fish bowl or in any combination of colors. Allow for seams. The block may have 8 sides or it may be square as one likes. If used for a pillow, use a strip 3″ or 4″ wide to box in the design.

From 1935: This is a requested pattern by the *Weekly Star*'s quilt fans. It has many names, the oldest being Dove in the Window. Gold Fish is a later name. Allow for seams.

From light blue fabric, cut:

- 4 pieces using pattern C

- 4 pieces using pattern E

- 4 pieces using pattern B

- 4 pieces using pattern D

From gold fabric, cut:

- 4 diamonds using pattern H

- 4 triangles using pattern F

- 4 triangles using pattern I

From brown fabric, cut:

- 4 diamonds using pattern G

- 4 triangles using pattern F

- 4 triangles using pattern I

To Make the Block

1. Stitch the I triangles to the light blue E pieces. Make 4.

2. Sew the F triangles to the light blue C pieces. Make 4.

3. Sew the G and H diamonds together in pairs. Then sew 2 pairs together. That makes up half of the center of the block. Sew the 2 halves together. Don't sew the seam entirely to the end as these will be inset seams.

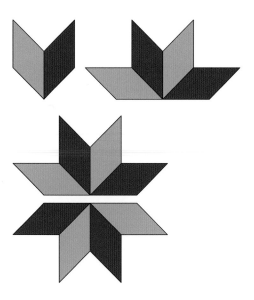

4. Inset the I-E-I units and the F-C-F units.

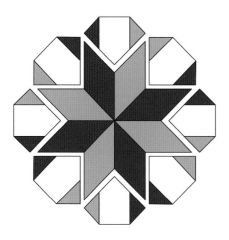

5. Inset the B and D light blue diamonds.

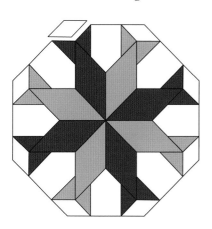

6. Add the A triangles to complete the block.

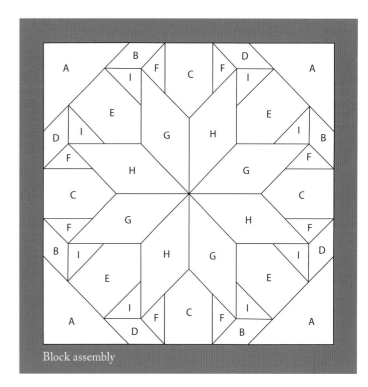

Block assembly

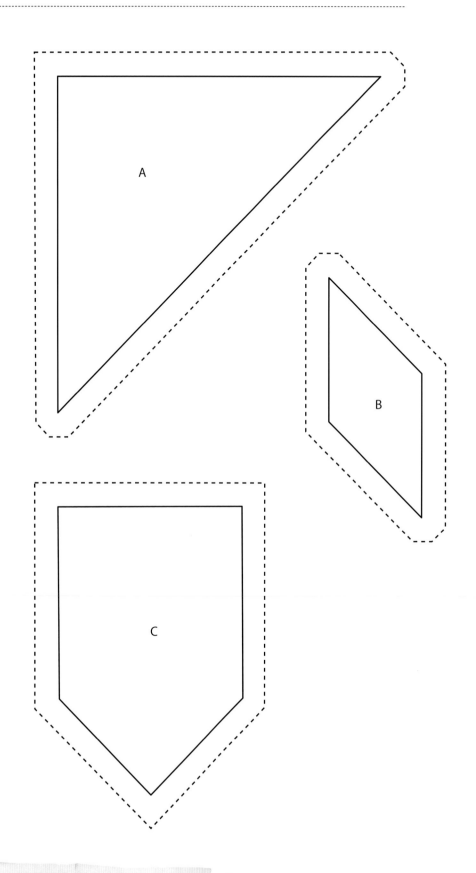

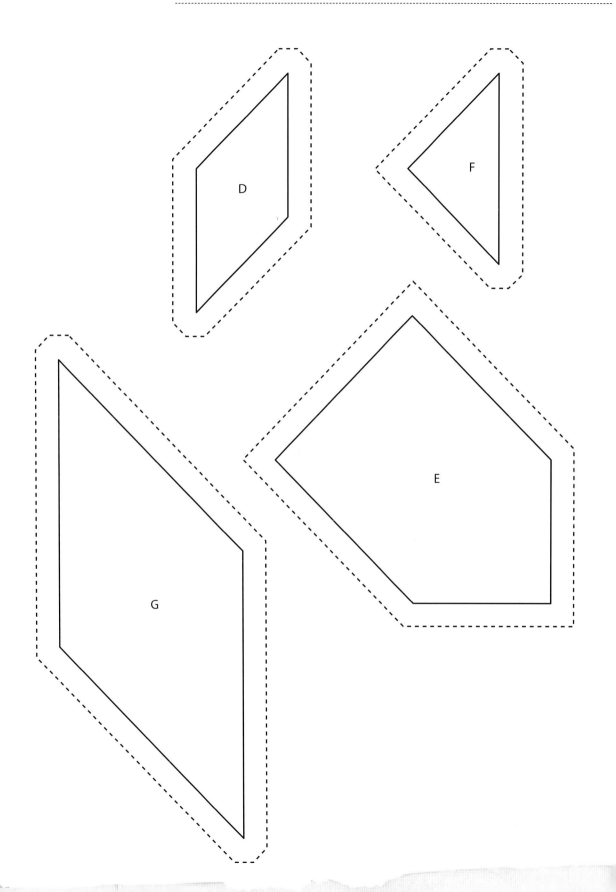

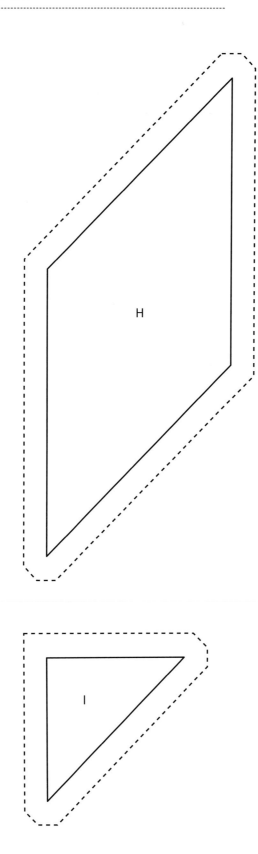

1931 Pontiac Star

Finished block: 12″ × 12″

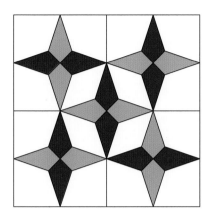

Fabric Needed

Dark blue • Medium blue • Cream

Cutting Instructions

Use the Pontiac Star patterns (page 73).

From dark blue fabric, cut:

• 10 pieces using pattern B

From medium blue fabric, cut:

• 10 pieces using pattern B

From cream fabric, cut:

• 12 pieces using pattern A

• 4 diamonds using pattern C

Newspaper Archive

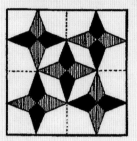

Appeared in *The Kansas City Star* on February 21, 1931 (block #158)

Original size: 12″. A simple lesson in quilting is the piecing of this very pretty star pattern called Pontiac Star because of its arrowhead motif. The stars are placed in an interesting arrangement. To make a perfect pattern, one should watch the position of these stars very carefully in putting the quilt together. The block is 12″ square and is alternated with plain material the same size. Allow for seams.

To Make the Block

1. Sew the medium blue and dark blue pieces together forming a star. Make 5.

2. Inset the cream A pieces to 3 outer edges of 4 of the stars.

3. Inset the cream A pieces to 3 outer edges of 4 of the stars.

4. Inset the cream A pieces to 3 outer edges of 4 of the stars.

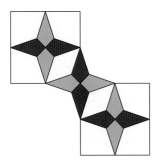

5. Add the upper right and lower left stars to complete the block.

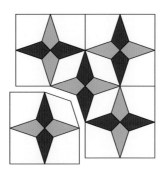

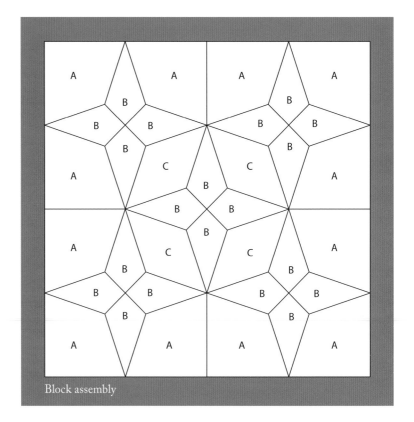

Block assembly

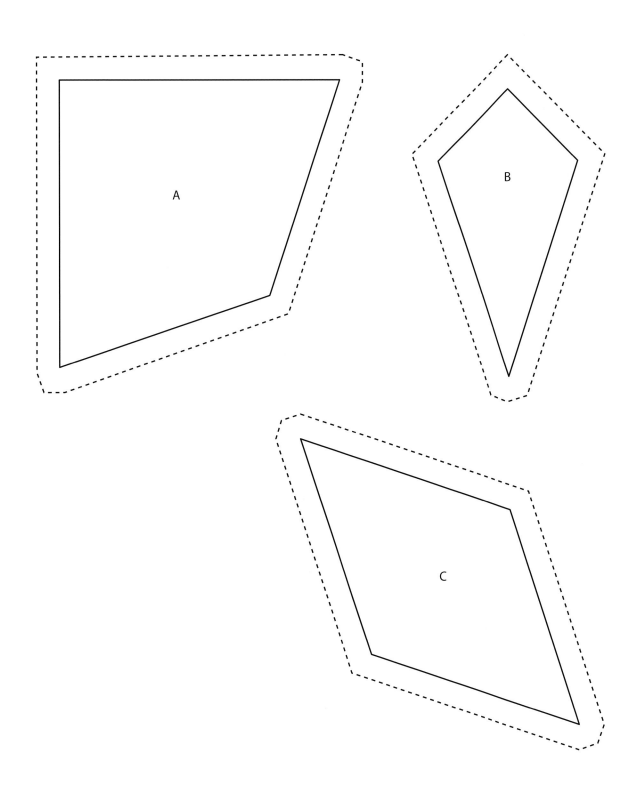

1932 Puss in the Corner

Finished block: 12″ × 12″

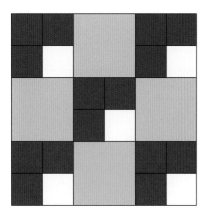

Fabric Needed

Light green print
Brown and pink print
Pink and green print

Cutting Instructions

Use the Puss in the Corner patterns (page 76). This block can also be made using a rotary cutter and ruler.

From light green print fabric, cut:

• 5 squares 2½″ × 2½″ (pattern A)

From brown and pink print fabric, cut:

• 15 squares 2½″ × 2½″ (pattern A)

From pink and green fabric, cut:

• 4 squares 4½″ × 4½″ (pattern B)

Newspaper Archive

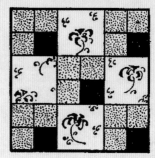

Appeared in *The Kansas City Star* on November 5, 1932 (block #270) and June 17, 1933 (block #310)

From 1932: What a cunning variation of the old-time nine-patch, and so easy to make, too. The charm of it lies in the unusual placing of the small dark squares. This makes a 12″ block, but if a daintier effect is desired, cut down the size. Allow seams.

From 1933: Several requests have come for a quilt which a little girl may piece during vacation. We look over our files and select Puss in the Corner as an easy pattern which makes a pretty quilt. Allow for seams. All edges are straight. This is a repeated pattern.

To Make the Block

1. Sew 2 brown A squares together and 1 brown and light green print square together. Sew the pairs together to make a four-patch unit. Make 5 units.

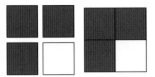

2. Sew the four-patch units and the squares together in rows to complete the block.

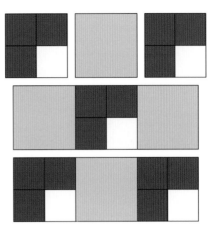

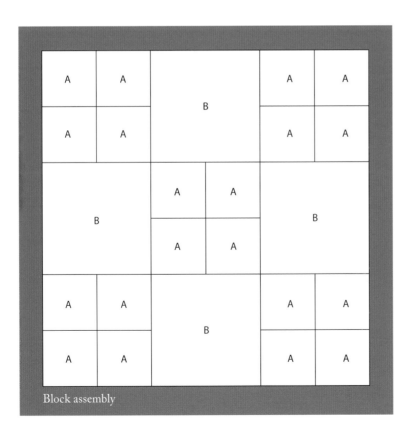

Block assembly

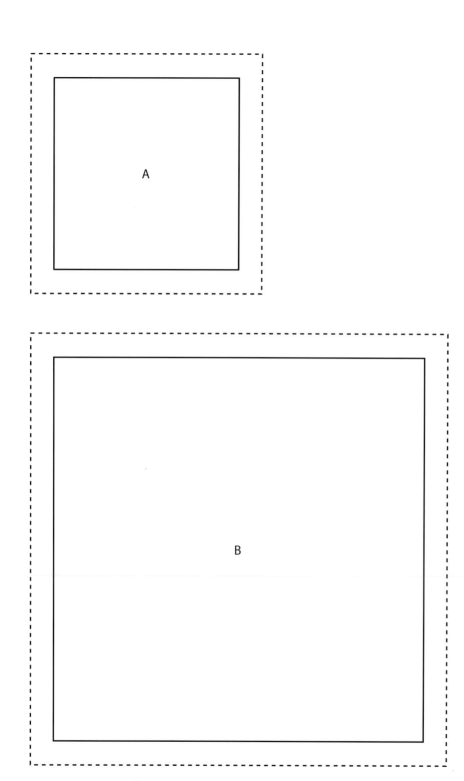

1932 Crazy Anne #1

Finished block: 12″ × 12″

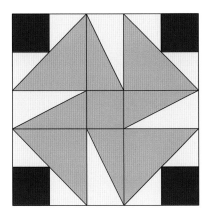

Fabric Needed

Dark orange • Light orange • Navy blue

Cutting Instructions

Use the Crazy Anne #2 patterns (pages 79–80).
This block can also be made using a rotary
cutter and ruler for the measured pieces.

From navy blue fabric, cut:

• 4 squares 2⅞″ × 2⅞″ (pattern A)

From light orange fabric, cut:

• 4 squares 3¼″ × 3¼″. Cut each square once on
the diagonal or cut 8 triangles using pattern B.

• 4 triangles using pattern C

Newspaper Archive

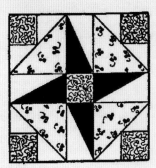

Appeared in *The Kansas City Star*
on October 15, 1932 (block #855)

This futuristic pattern is so prophetic
of the latest trend in decorative
design as to be quite startling, yet it
is one of our great-grandmother's
favorites. While 3 colors are shown,
2 are equally interesting and give an
entirely different effect. This is not a
difficult block to piece as the rows are
so well defined and the edges straight.
It is 12″ square and will be alternated
with plain blocks of the same size. No
seams are allowed.

From dark orange fabric, cut:

• 4 triangles using pattern C

• 1 square 2⅞″ × 2⅞″ (pattern A)

• 2 squares 5⅝″ × 5⅝″. Cut each square once on
the diagonal or cut 4 triangles using pattern D.

To Make the Block

1. If using squares instead of patterns, take a scant ¼″ seam allowance so the finished block will be 12″ square.

Sew 2 light orange triangles to a blue square. Then add a dark orange D triangle.

2. Stitch the dark orange and light orange C triangles together. You should have 4 units.

3. Sew the block together in rows.

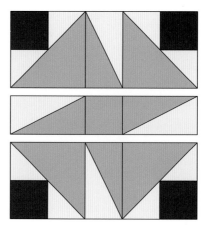

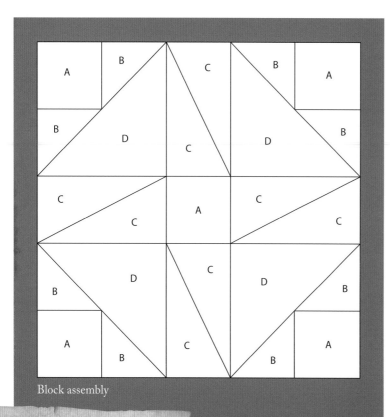

Block assembly

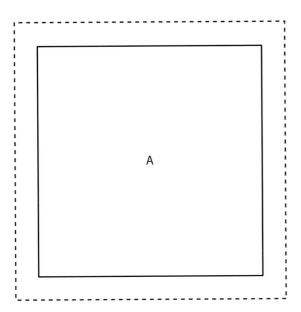

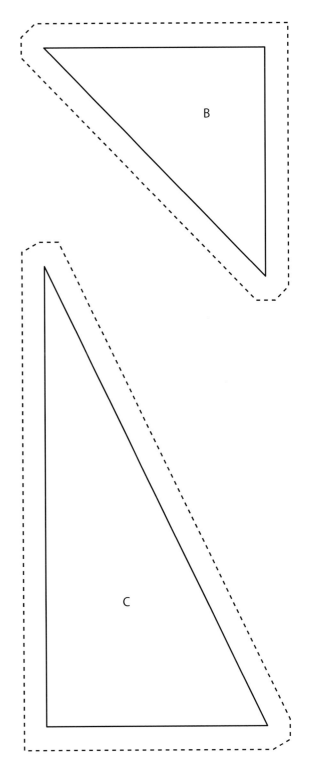

A

B

C

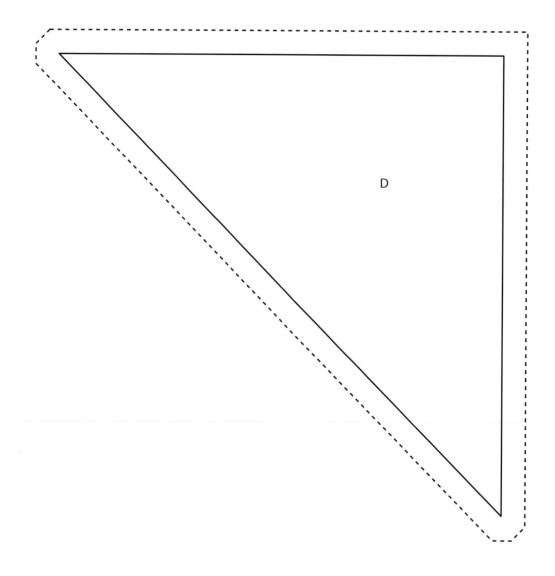

D

1932 Hearts Desire

Finished block: 12″ × 12″

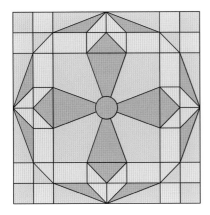

Fabric Needed

Blue • Medium orange • Light orange

Cutting Instructions

Use the Hearts Desire patterns (pages 84–85).
NOTE: A seam has been added to make this easier to piece.

From medium orange, cut:

- 4 pieces using pattern J
- 4 triangles using pattern G
- 4 pieces using pattern F
- 4 pieces using pattern I
- 1 circle using pattern K

From light orange, cut:

- 20 triangles using pattern E
- 8 rectangles using pattern D
- 8 squares using pattern A

From blue, cut:

- 4 squares using pattern A
- 4 triangles using pattern E
- 4 triangles using pattern B
- 4 triangles using pattern C
- 4 triangles using pattern H

To Make the Block

1. Sew the light orange E triangles to the blue E triangles thus making 4 half-square triangles. Set these aside for the moment.

2. Sew the center of the block together by pairing piece H to piece J. You need to make 4 pairs.

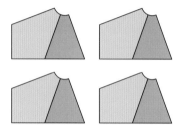

3. Make half of the center of the block by sewing 2 pairs together. Sew the 2 halves together.

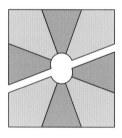

4. Baste the center circle in place to stabilize the block. You'll want to actually appliqué that piece in place last.

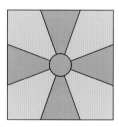

5. To make the outer part of the block, sew an E triangle to each side of triangle G. Add a D rectangle. Make 4.

6. Sew a blue C triangle to an orange I triangle. Now add a light orange E triangle.

7. Sew the orange F triangle to the blue B triangle. Add a light E triangle. Sew the 2 pieces together. Make 4.

8. Sew the 2 rows together.

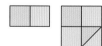

9. Now make four-patch units by sewing a light orange A square to the blue/light orange half-square triangle.

10. Sew a blue A square to a light orange A square. Sew the 4 squares together. Make 4.

11. Sew the block together in rows.

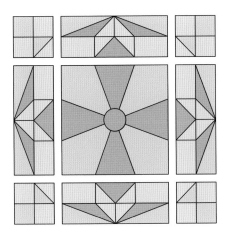

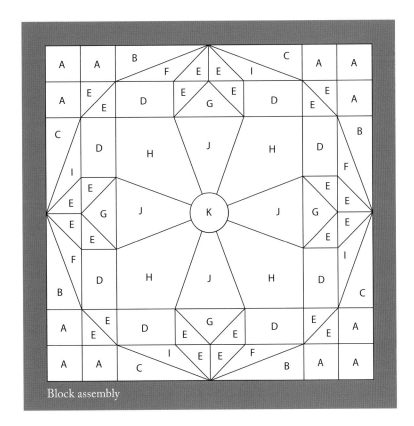

Block assembly

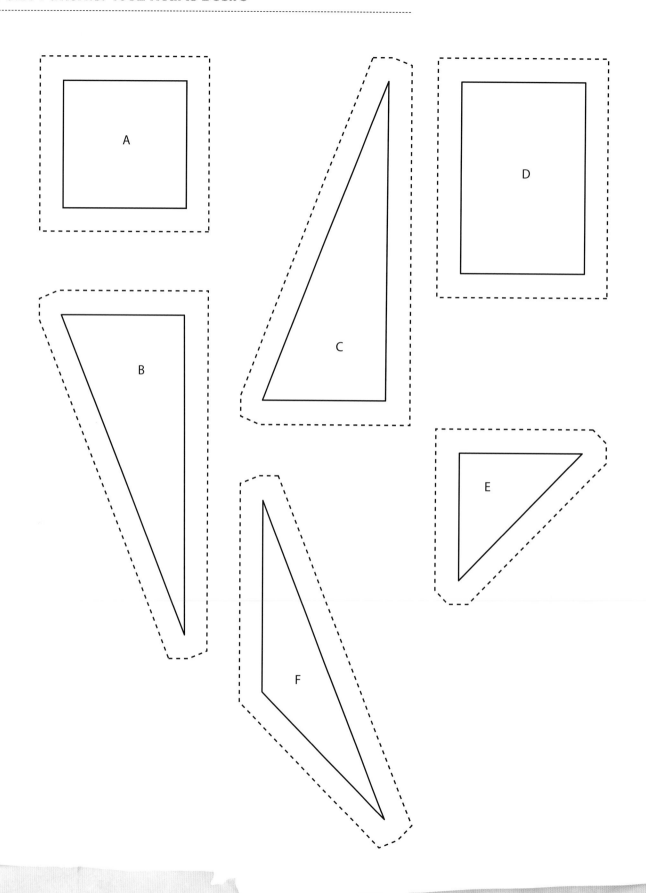

A

B

C

D

E

F

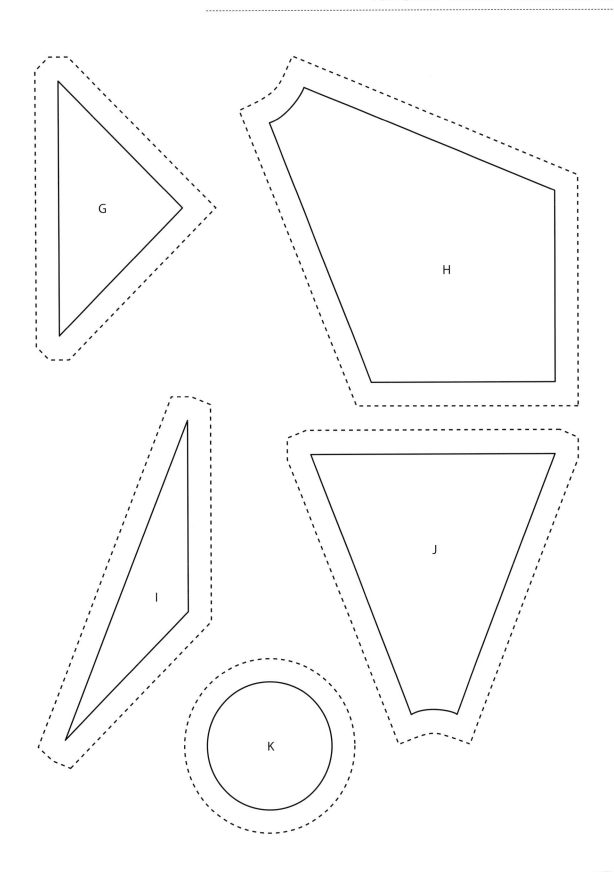

1932 Garden Maze

Finished block: 12″ × 12″

Fabric Needed

Green • Pink • Cream • Pink and green print
(This can be a large scale floral if you choose.)

Cutting Instructions

Use the Garden Maze patterns (pages 88–89).
This block can also be made using a rotary
cutter and ruler for the measured piece.

From pink, cut:

• 2 pieces using pattern C

• 4 pieces using pattern A

• 4 pieces using pattern D

From green fabric, cut:

• 2 pieces using pattern C

• 4 pieces using pattern A

• 4 pieces using pattern D

From cream fabric, cut:

• 4 pieces using pattern E

• 16 pieces using pattern B

From pink and green print, cut:

• 1 square 4½″ × 4½″ (pattern F)

Newspaper Archive

Appeared in *The Kansas City Star*
on May 28, 1932 (block #244)

Original size: 12″, pieced. This intricate
pattern is one of the most beautiful of all
the old quilt designs, and a great favorite of
our grandmothers. They usually employed
2 colors, light and dark. A more modern
development is to use a single flower center
for each 4″ square, either all alike or all
different, then choose a striped or trailing
vine effect for the pieces marked rose. The
lattice is green. The result is charming.
Note that a section of quilt is shown, not
a block as this pattern must be a building
up of row after row until the desired size is
reached. Allow seams.

To Make the Block

1. Sew the green, pink and cream D and E rectangles together. Make 4.

2. Sew a cream B triangle to either side of a green A piece. Make 4.

3. Sew a green/cream AB piece to a pink C piece. Make 2.

4. Sew a cream B triangle to either side of a pink A piece. Make 4.

5. Sew a pink/cream AB piece to a green C piece. Make 2.

6. Sew the corner pieces to a rectangle unit. Make 1 row like this.

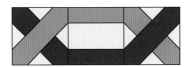

7. Make 1 row like this.

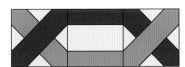

8. Make the center row by sewing a rectangle unit to either side of the center square.

9. Sew the rows together to complete the block.

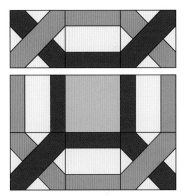

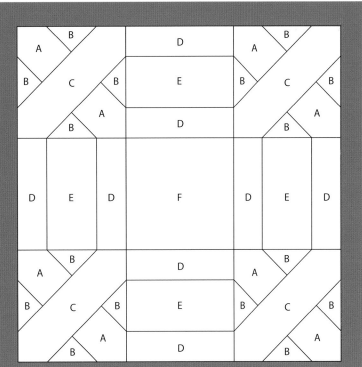

Block assembly

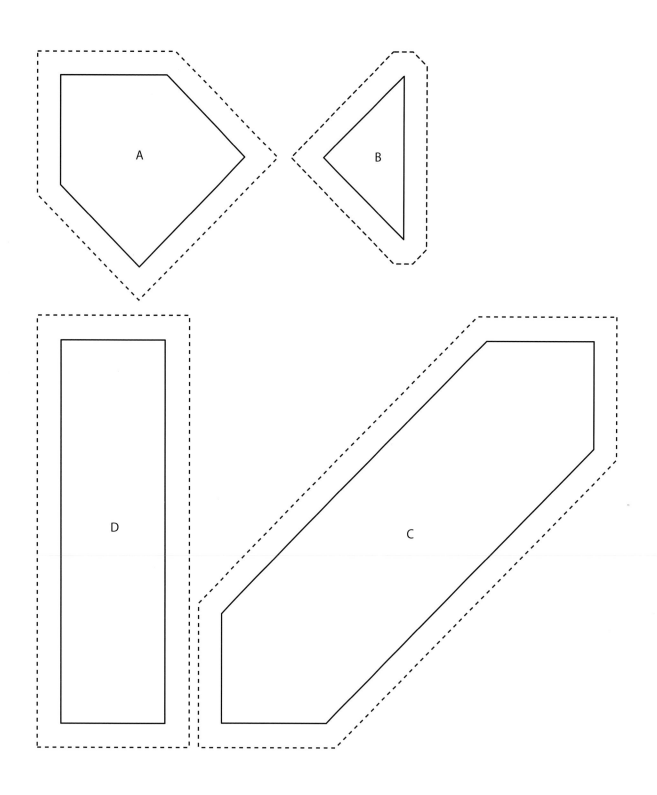

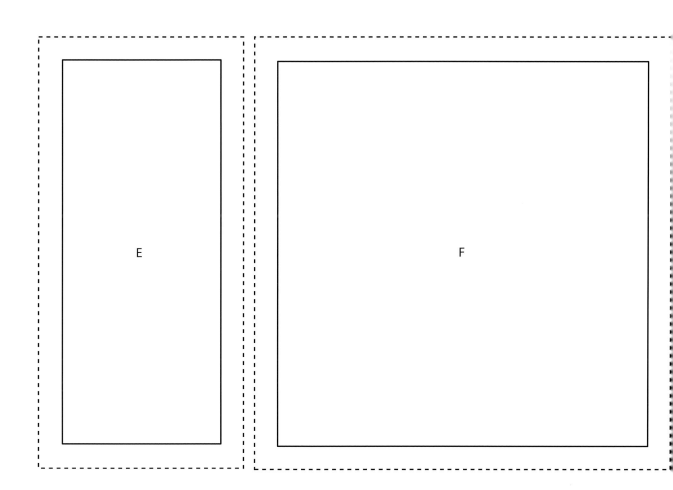

1933 Economy

Finished block: 12″ × 12″

Fabric Needed

Light tan • Medium tan
Dark brown • Dark red

Cutting Instructions

Use the Economy patterns (page 92). This block can also be made using a rotary cutter and ruler.

From light tan, cut:

• 34 squares 1⅞″ × 1⅞″. Cut each square once from corner to corner on the diagonal to make 68 triangles (pattern A).

From medium tan, cut:

• 16 rectangles 2½″ × 1½″ (pattern B)

From dark brown, cut:

• 4 rectangles 2½″ × 5½″ (pattern C)

• 4 squares 1½″ × 1½″ (pattern D)

Newspaper Archive

Appeared in *The Kansas City Star* on August 12, 1933 (block #318)

After the other quilts are finished and the basket is full of scraps then is the time to start the Economy quilt. Colors will necessarily be heterogeneous but the block-effect of the quilt will give plenty of opportunity for variety.

From dark red, cut:

• 17 squares 1¹⁵⁄₁₆″ × 1¹⁵⁄₁₆″ (pattern E) (Or cut 2″ squares and use a generous ¼″ seam allowance.)

To Make the Block

1. Sew the A triangles to the E squares. You need 17 A-E units.

2. Sew an A-E unit to either side of a medium tan B rectangle. Make 8 strips.

3. Sew a B rectangle to either side of a dark brown D square. Make 4 strips.

4. To make the 4 corners of the block, sew the strips together. Make 4 corner units.

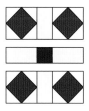

5. Sew a corner unit to either side of a dark brown C rectangle. Make 2 strips.

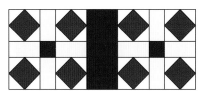

6. Sew a dark brown C rectangle to either side of an A-E unit.

7. Sew the strips together to complete the block.

Block assembly

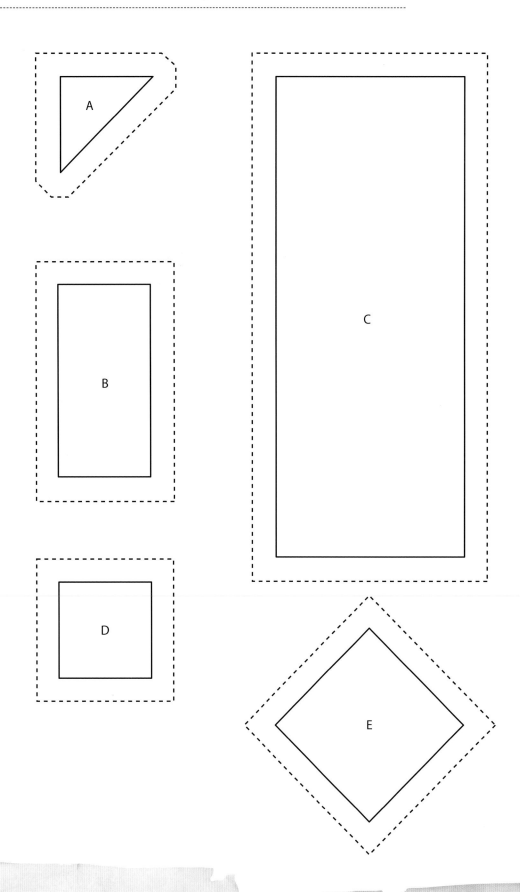

A

B

C

D

E

1933 Triplet

Finished block: 12″ × 12″

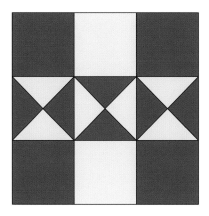

Fabric Needed

Light blue • Dark blue

Cutting Instructions

Use the Triplet patterns (page 95). This block can also be made using a rotary cutter and ruler.

From light blue fabric, cut:

- 2 squares 4½″ × 4½″ (pattern A)

- 2 squares 5¼″ × 5¼″. Cut each square twice on the diagonal to make 8 triangles. You will have 2 triangles left over. Or cut 6 triangles using pattern B.

From dark blue fabric, cut:

- 4 squares 4½″ × 4½″ (pattern A)

- 2 squares 5¼″ × 5¼″. Cut each square twice on the diagonal to make 8 triangles. You will have 2 triangles left over. Or cut 6 triangles using pattern B.

Newspaper Archive

Appeared in *The Kansas City Star* on August 19, 1933 (block #319)

Original size: 12″, pieced. An interesting cross arrangement that makes up prettily in dark and light colors is the Triplet quilt block which was sent in by Polli J. Redford of Urich, Missouri. The 3 center blocks may be varied as one pleases, a nice combination being to use half dark triangles and half light and alternating their position in the block. The 2 large square blocks are of light fabric.

To Make the Block

1. Sew 4 B triangles together. Make 3 of these quarter-square triangle units.

2. Sew the squares together alternating the dark blue and light blue. Make 2 rows.

3. Sew the quarter-square triangles together. Make 1 row.

4. Sew the 3 rows together to complete the block.

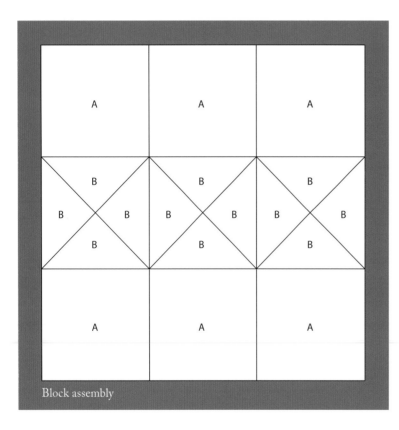

Block assembly

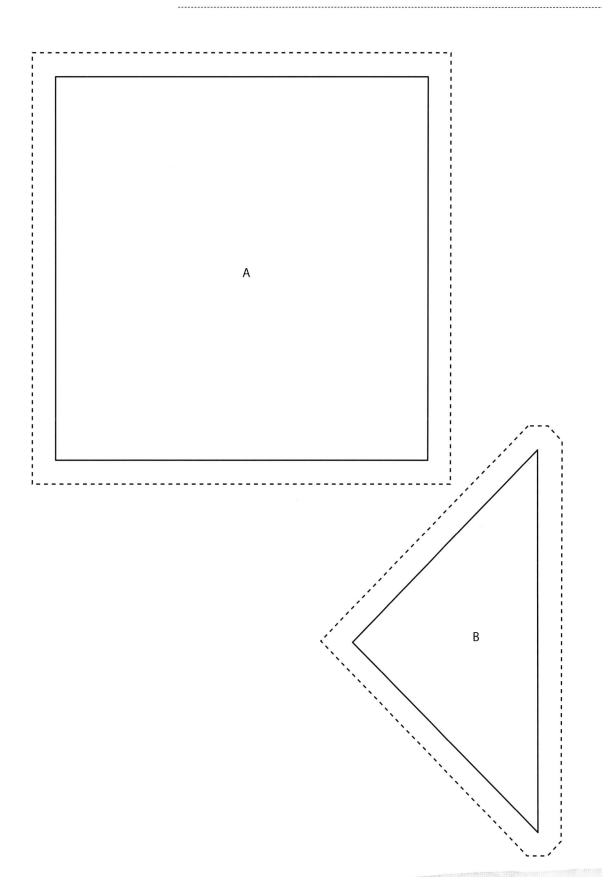

A

B

1933 Charm Quilt

Finished piece: 3″ × 4¼″

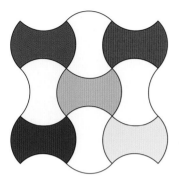

Fabric Needed

Light and dark scraps

Cutting Instructions

Use the Charm Quilt pattern (page 97).

NOTE: You do not make a block per se when making this quilt; instead you would determine how many pieces it would take to make 1 row the width of the quilt you want to make, and then make as many rows as necessary to complete the quilt to the desired length.

Newspaper Archive

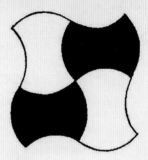

Appeared in *The Kansas City Star* on December 30, 1933 (block #382)

Original size: 6″ × 4¼″, pieced. This quilt may be made in 2 colors or in white and prints. It is an allover quilt pattern and one that is easily cut, but must be sewed with even seams and small stitches. Piece in blocks of 4 pieces and set all together. Allow for seams. This was contributed by Mrs. A. Herrick of Edison, Missouri, who has used many Star quilt patterns. Thank you, Mrs. Herrick.

To Make the Block

1. Sew the pieces into rows, alternating light and dark pieces. Begin the row with a horizontal piece then add a piece that is oriented vertically. Continue in this manner until the row is the desired width, making sure the row ends with a piece that is horizontal.

2. Begin the next row with a piece that is oriented vertically, then add a horizontal piece. Continue until your have enough pieces sewn together to make a row, making sure the row ends with a piece that is vertical.

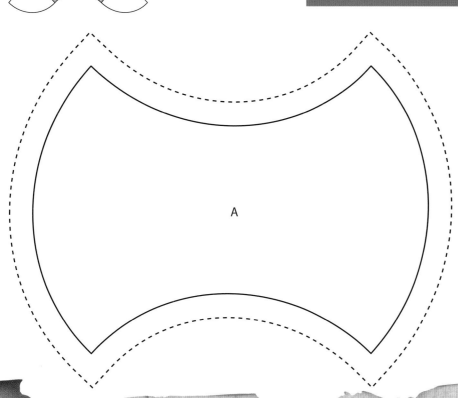

3. Continue to make alternating rows until your quilt top is the desired size. No borders are necessary for this quilt. You would simply layer it with backing and batting and quilt it. Then bind the edges with bias binding for a pretty finish.

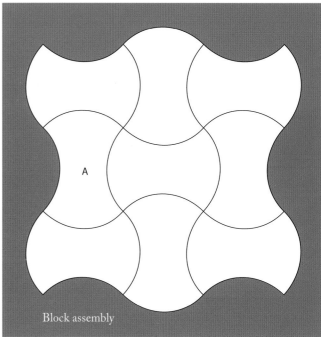

Block assembly

A

1934 Red Cross

Finished block: 12″ × 12″

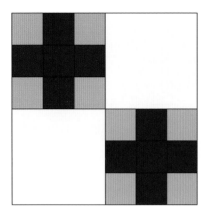

Fabric Needed

Tan • Cream • Red

NOTE: This block was originally intended to honor the Red Cross, but you can, of course, use colors of your choice.

Cutting Instructions

Use the Red Cross patterns (page 100). This block can also be made using a rotary cutter and ruler.

From tan fabric, cut:

• 8 squares 2½″ × 2½″ (pattern A)

From cream fabric, cut:

• 2 squares 6½″ × 6½″ (pattern B)

From red fabric, cut:

• 10 squares 2½″ × 2½″ (pattern A)

Newspaper Archive

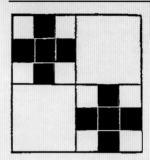

Appeared in *The Kansas City Star* on July 21, 1934 (block #363)

Original size: 8¼″, pieced. A Kansas City quilt fan who worked for the Red Cross during the World War knitting and wrapping bandages sent this attractive block which may be done in red and white and set together with white squares which may be quilted with patriotic emblems—the flag, the eagle, the crossed swords, the outline of the Liberty Memorial. Many quilt fans will think of others as they plan the plain blocks.

To Make the Block

1. Sew a tan square to either side of a red square. Make 4 rows.

2. Sew 3 red squares together. Make 2 rows.

3. Sew the rows together into 2 sets of 3.

4. Complete the block by sewing the large cream 6½″ squares and the pieced squares together.

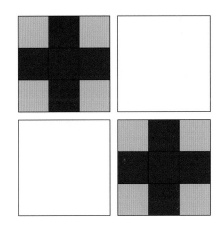

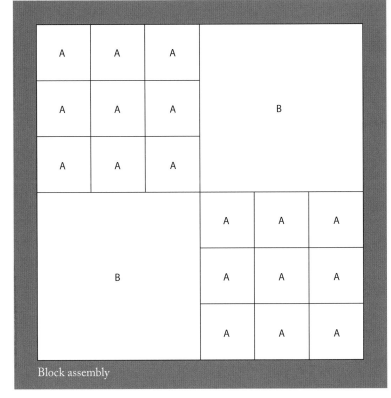

Block assembly

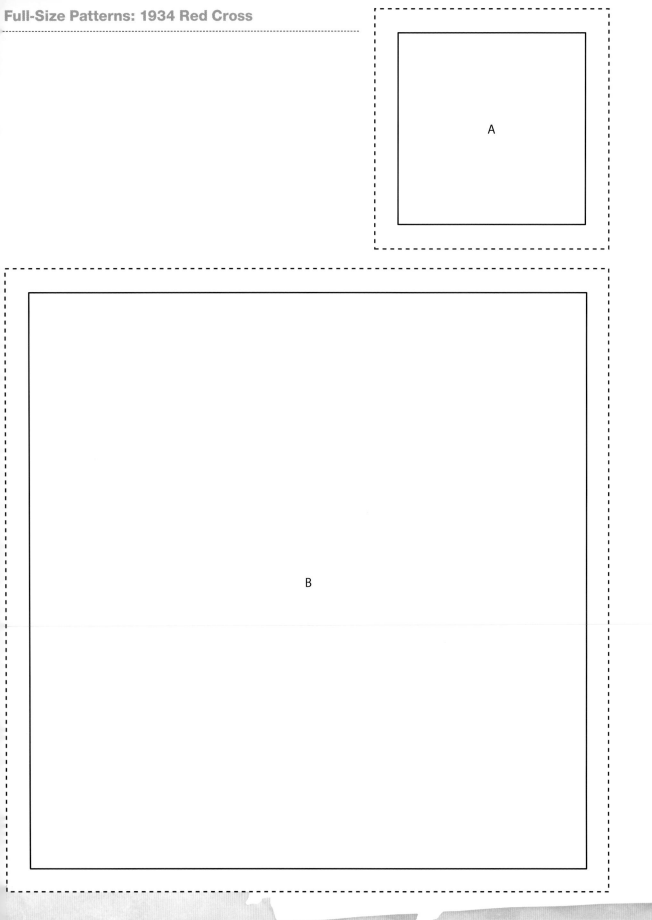

A

B

1935 Arkansas Snowflake

Finished block: 6″ × 6″

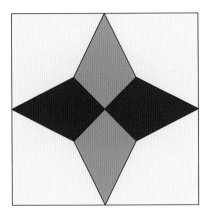

Fabric Needed

Background • Teal • Purple

Cutting Instructions

Use the Arkansas Snowflake patterns (page 103).

From background fabric, cut:

• 4 pieces using pattern A

From teal fabric, cut:

• 2 pieces using pattern B

From purple fabric, cut:

• 2 pieces using pattern B

Newspaper Archive

Appeared in *The Kansas City Star* on February 9, 1935 (block #388)

This pattern, called the Arkansas Star or the Snow Flake, is one that a child can do. The completed quilt is lovely in print and plain blocks on white or pale lemon background. It was contributed by a quilt fan, Mrs. J. L. Wiesle of Brinkley, Arkansas.

To Make the Block

1. Sew a purple B piece to a teal B piece. Make 2. Don't sew all the way to the end of the seams as they will be inset later.

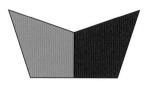

2. Sew the 2 units together. Don't sew all the way to the end of the seams as they will be inset later.

3. Inset the 4 background B pieces to complete the block.

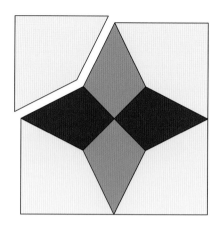

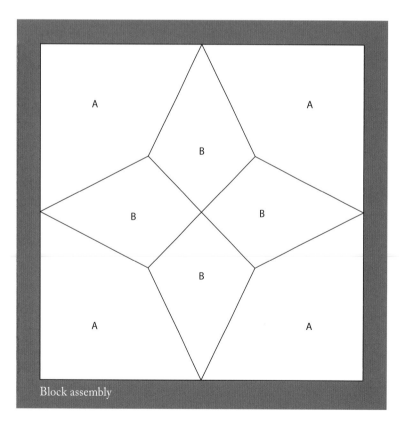

Block assembly

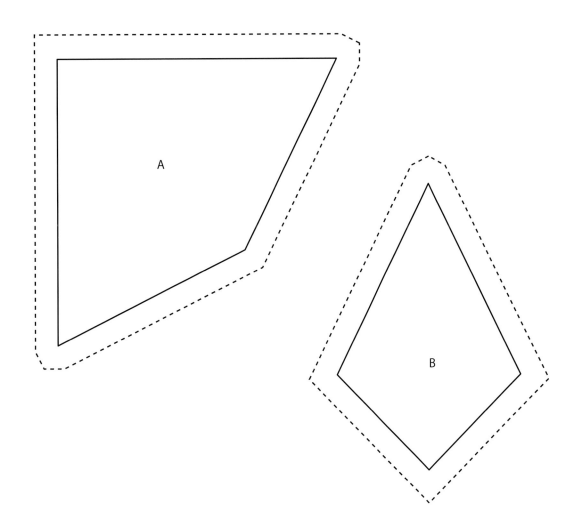

A

B

1935 Railroad Crossing

Finished block: 12″ × 12″

Fabric Needed

Red • Cream

Cutting Instructions

Use the Railroad Crossing patterns (pages 106–107). This block can also be made using a rotary cutter and ruler.

NOTE: If you are cutting your pieces using a rotary cutter and ruler, you will need to use a scant ¼″ seam allowance when sewing.

From cream-colored fabric, cut:

• 1 square 8¼″ × 8¼″. Cut the square from corner to corner twice on the diagonal or cut 4 triangles using pattern B.

• 4 rectangles 1⅝″ × 5⅜″ (pattern C)

Newspaper Archive

Appeared in *The Kansas City Star* on August 21, 1935 (block #415)

Original size: 10½″. Here is a quilt which many quilt fans call a "straight line quilt," as it has no curved seams. It is a striking quilt in prints with a plain color of the same tone.

From red fabric, cut:

• 8 rectangles 1⅝″ × 5⅜″ (pattern C)

• 1 square 4″ × 4″ (pattern D)

• 2 squares 3⅜″ × 3⅜″. Cut the squares from corner to corner once on the diagonal or cut 4 triangles using pattern A.

To Make the Block

1. Sew the C rectangles together. Make 4.

2. Sew a cream B triangle to either side of 2 of the rectangle units.

3. Sew a rectangle unit to either side of the center square.

4. Sew the 3 units together.

5. Add the A triangles to the 4 corners to complete the block.

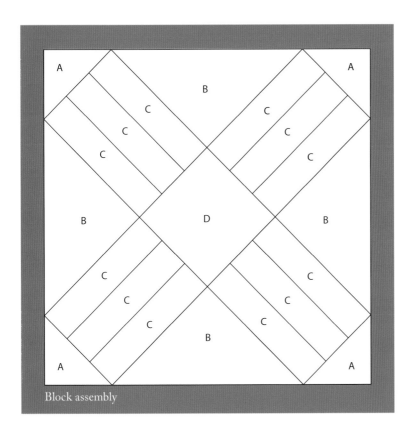

Block assembly

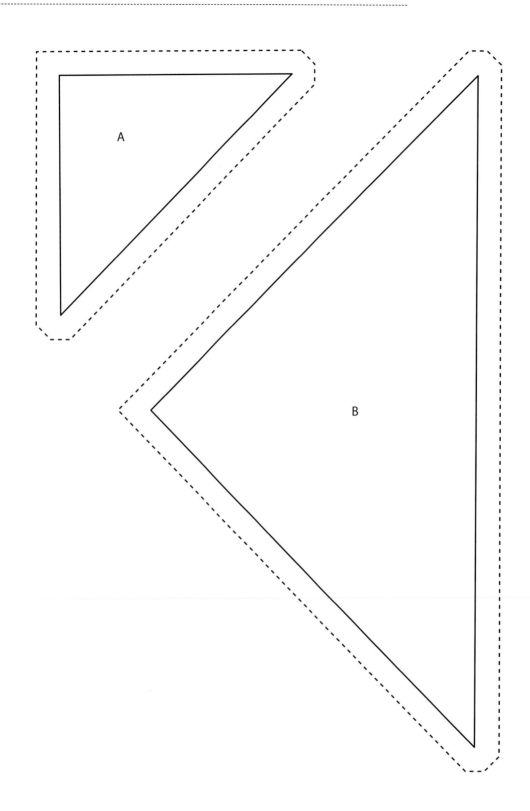

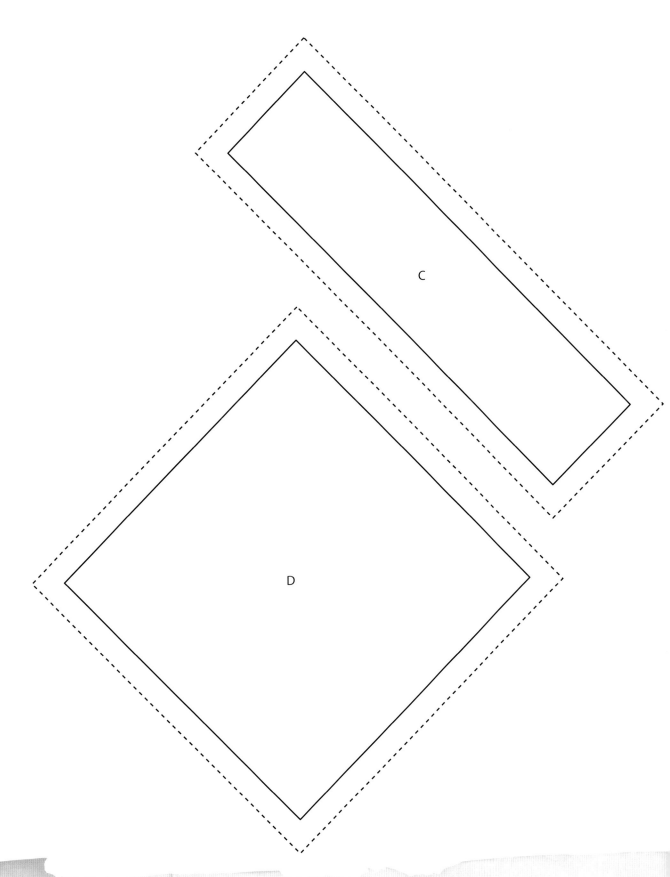

C

D

1935 Bridle Path

Finished block: 12″ × 12″

Fabric Needed

Dark red print • Pink/red print • Gray

Cutting Instructions

Use the Bridle Path patterns (page 110). This block can also be made using a rotary cutter and ruler.

From gray fabric, cut:

- 4 squares 3⅞″ × 3⅞″ or cut 8 triangles using pattern B

- 32 squares 1½″ × 1½″ or use pattern A

From dark red print, cut:

- 4 squares 3⅞″ × 3⅞″ or cut 8 triangles using pattern B

- 20 squares 1½″ × 1½″ or use pattern A

From pink/red print, cut:

- 20 squares 1½″ × 1½″ or use pattern A

Newspaper Archive

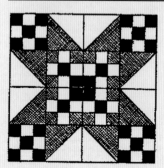

Appeared in *The Kansas City Star* on March 9, 1935 (block #392)

Original size: 16″. These large blocks make an attractive quilt. The "path" is traced by the dark blocks. This quilt design was contributed by Gladys Simmons of Grand Pass, Missouri.

To Make the Block

1. You will need to make half-square triangle units for this block.

To make half-square triangles, draw a line from corner to corner on the diagonal on the reverse side of the lightest fabric. Place a light square atop a darker square and sew ¼″ on each side of the line. Use your rotary cutter and cut on the line. Open each unit and press toward the darkest fabric.

Make 8 dark red print/gray half-square triangles. Set aside.

2. Sew the pink/red print 1½″ squares and the gray 1½″ squares together to make nine-patch blocks. Make 4.

3. Sew the dark red print 1½″ squares and the gray 1½″ squares together to make nine-patch blocks. Make 4.

4. Sew the half-square triangle units and the nine-patch units into rows.

5. Sew the rows together to complete the block.

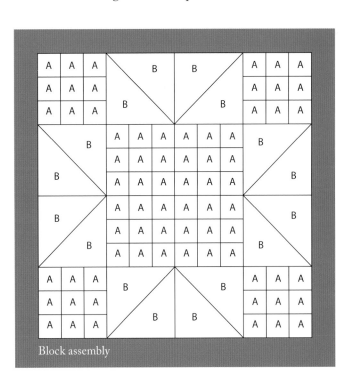

Block assembly

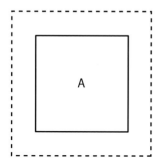

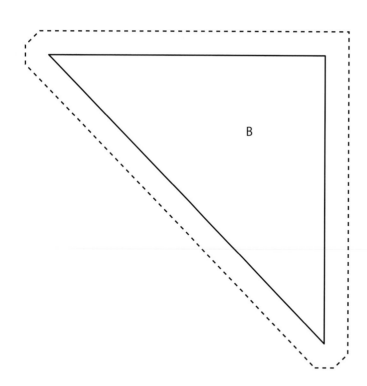

1935 Arabic Lattice

Finished block: 12″ × 12″

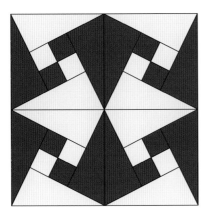

Fabric Needed

Brown • Cream

Cutting Instructions

Use the Arabic Lattice patterns (page 113).

From brown fabric, cut:

- 4 pieces using pattern A
- 4 pieces using pattern B
- 8 squares using pattern C

From cream fabric, cut:

- 4 pieces using pattern A
- 4 pieces using pattern B
- 8 squares using pattern C

Newspaper Archive

Appeared in *The Kansas City Star* on January 5, 1935 (block #384) and March 27, 1935 (block #394)

Original size: 5½″.

From January 1935: This quilt pattern is simple in the individual units as you see, but gives the impression of an intricate pattern when set together. Allow for seams.

From March 1935: This odd pattern is repeated by request. The individual blocks are simple. Allow for seams.

To Make the Block

1. Sew 2 cream C squares to 2 brown C squares to make a four-patch unit. Make 4.

2. Sew a cream A piece to the center four-patch unit. Notice that piece A extends past the four-patch unit. On this first seam, you need to stop sewing when you reach the midway point of the second square. Leave the remainder of the seam open.

Stop sewing where shown.

3. Now add a brown A piece.

4. Now a cream A piece to the top.

5. Sew a brown A piece to the left side. Go back and close up the first seamline. This is one-fourth of the block. Make 2.

6. Using the same technique as above, make 2 quadrants of the block using the brown and cream B pieces around the four-patch unit.

7. Sew the 4 quadrants together to complete the block.

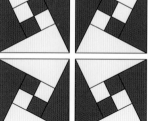

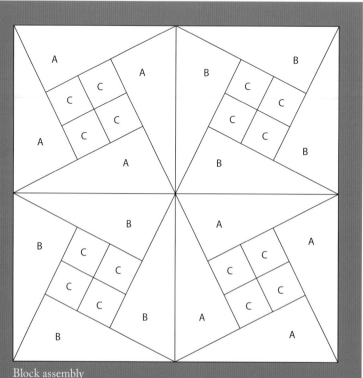

Block assembly

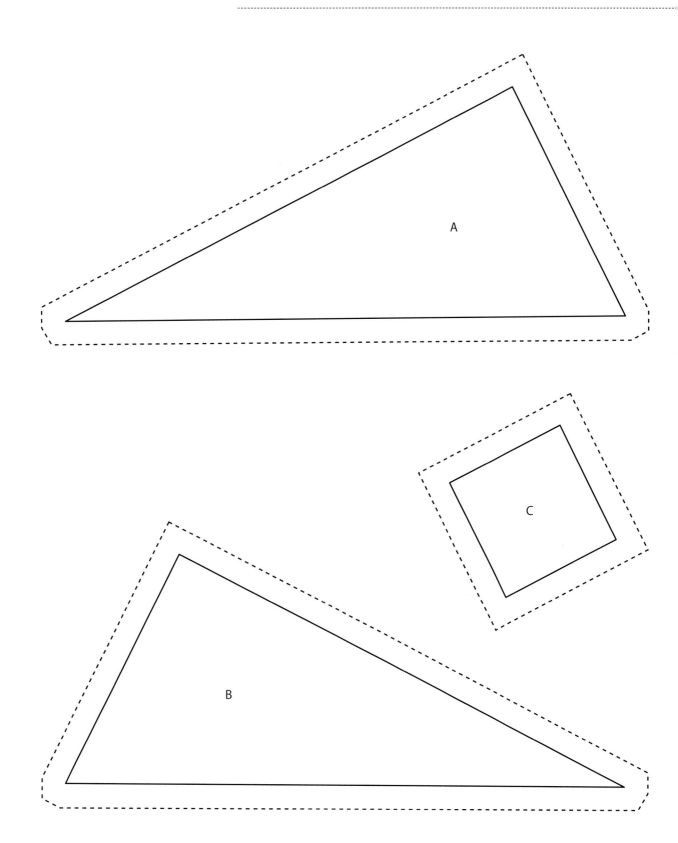

1936 Turkey Tracks

Finished block: 12″ × 12″

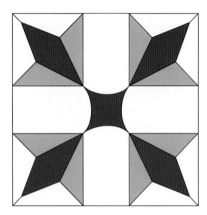

Fabric Needed

Dark • Medium • Light

Cutting Instructions

Use the Turkey Tracks patterns (page 117–118).

From light fabric, cut:

* 4 pieces using pattern B

* 4 pieces using pattern A

* 4 pieces using pattern C

From medium fabric, cut:

* 4 pieces using pattern D

* 4 pieces using pattern E

From dark fabric, cut:

* 4 diamonds using pattern F

* 1 piece using pattern G

Newspaper Archive

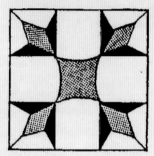

Appeared in *The Kansas City Star* on June 13, 1936 (block #459)

This pattern was the inspiration for the quilt series in *The Star*. It was the first pattern offered in this series sketched from a quilt at *The Star*'s Better Homes Show in 1928. There are many variations of the Turkey Track block and here is one that is pieced differently from the usual pattern. It was contributed by Ollie Wainwright of French, Arkansas.

To Make the Block

1. Before you begin sewing, mark your seam-lines. It is crucial that you do not sew beyond the ¼″ seamline. Sew a medium D piece to a dark F diamond, then add the medium E piece to the other side.

2. Pin, then sew the A piece to the diamond. Begin sewing at the top of the diamond and sew toward the E piece. Do not sew beyond the ¼″ seam allowance. Sew the seam between the A piece and the E piece closed. This will work best if you sew toward the diamond. Again, do not sew beyond the ¼″ seam allowance.

3. Add the C piece next using the same technique. Remove the piece from beneath the sewing machine foot. Start at the outside corner and sew the mitered seam in toward the diamond stopping before you sew into the ¼″ seam allowance. Make 4 of these corner units.

4. Sew a corner unit to a B piece, then add another corner unit. Make 2 rows.

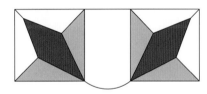

5. Sew a B piece to either side of the G piece. Make 1 row.

6. Sew the 3 rows together to complete the block

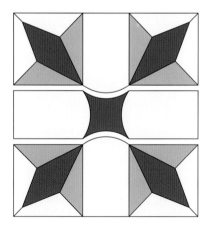

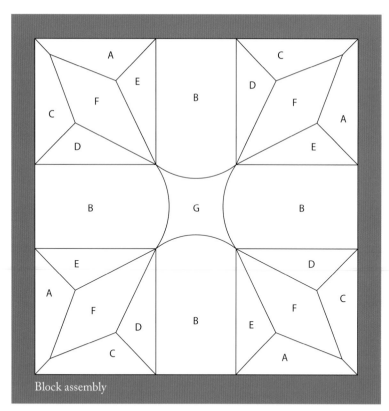

Block assembly

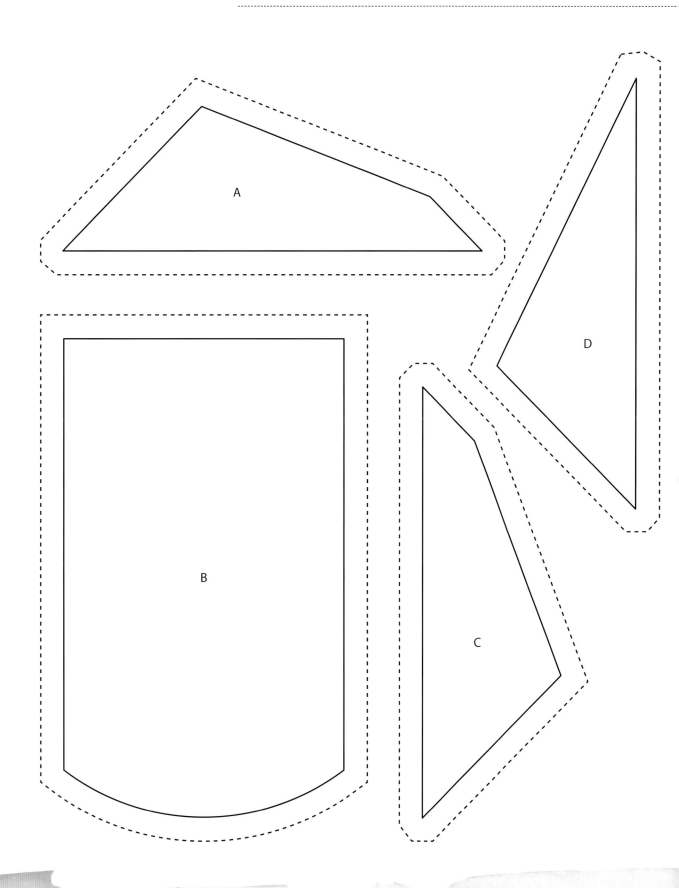

A

B

C

D

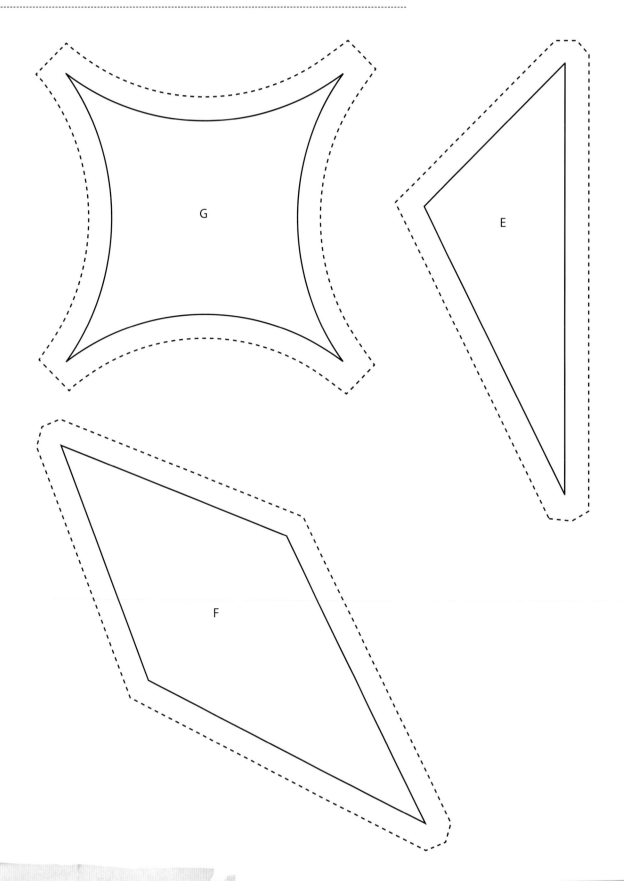

1936 White Lily

Finished block: 12″ × 12″

Fabric Needed

Scraps of different whites • Dark blue • Green

Cutting Instructions

Use the White Lily patterns (pages 122–124). This block can also be made using a rotary cutter and ruler for the measured piece.

From dark blue fabric, cut:

- 4 squares 4″ × 4″ (pattern A)
- 1 square 6¼″ × 6¼″. Cut the square twice on the diagonal or cut 3 triangles using pattern B. (If you cut the square, you will have 1 triangle left over.)
- 1 piece using pattern C

From white fabric, cut:

- 3 diamonds using pattern D
- 3 diamonds using pattern E

From green fabric, cut:

- 1 leaf using pattern G
- 1 stem using pattern F

Newspaper Archive

Appeared in *The Kansas City Star* on February 8, 1936 (block #441)

The White Lily pattern was contributed by Miss Vernetta Plummar of Brumley, Missouri. She points out this block can be pieced in 2 ways—by patching together the whole 9″ square and using all the pieces, or by putting the 6 diamond-shaped petals together and appliquéing them on the square.

To Make the Block

1. Sew 4 of the white diamonds together in pairs.

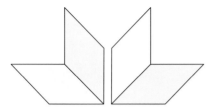

2. Inset a blue A square to the 2 pairs of diamonds

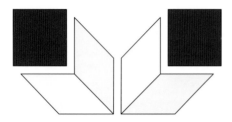

3. Inset a blue B triangle and stitch the units together.

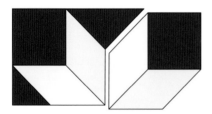

4. Appliqué the F stem to the C piece. Sew a diamond to either side of the top of piece C.

5. Inset a blue A square.

6. Sew the top of the block to the bottom and inset the 2 remaining B triangles.

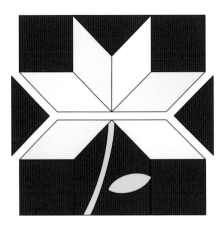

7. Appliqué the leaf in place to complete the block.

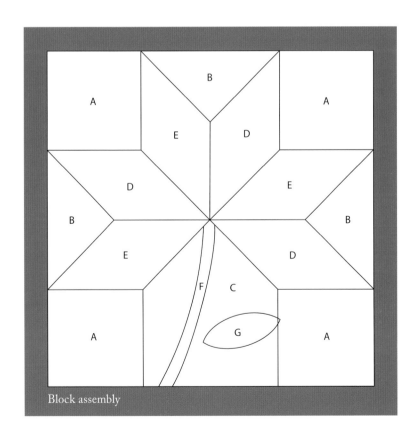

Block assembly

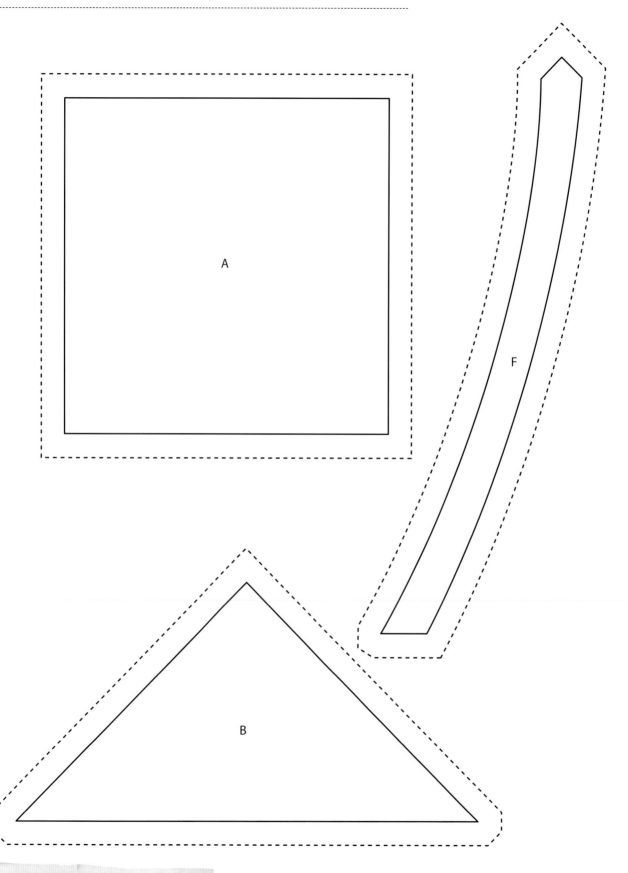

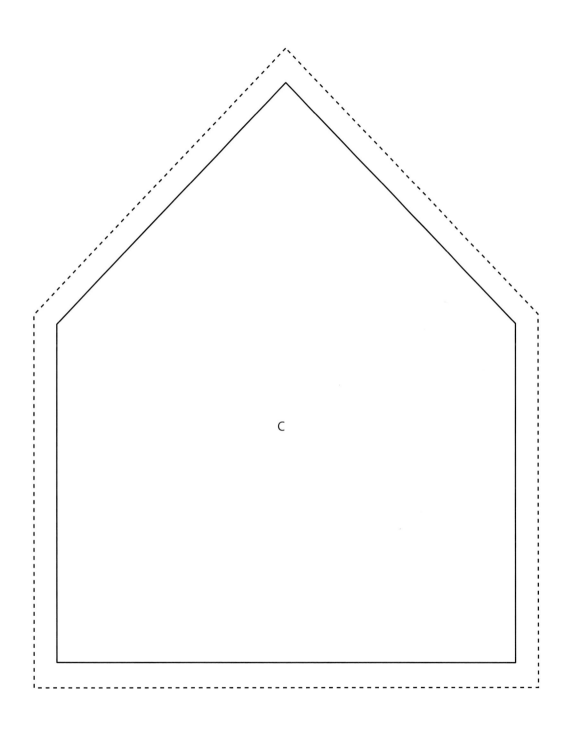

C

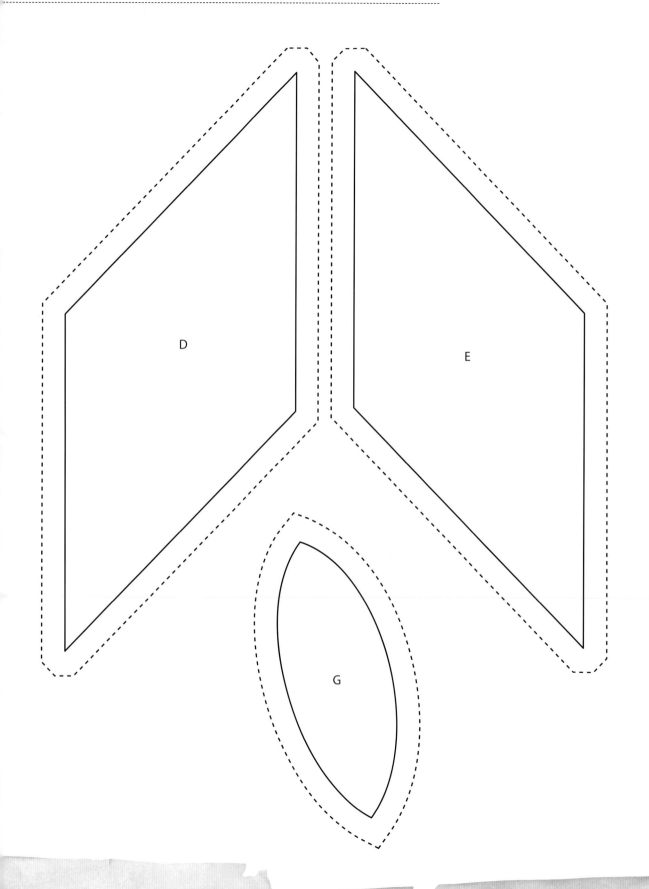

1937 Depression

Finished block: 12″ × 12″

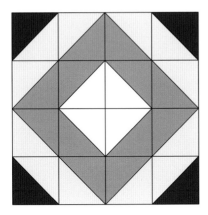

Fabric Needed

Light blue • Medium blue
Blue print • Dark blue

Cutting Instructions

Use the Depression pattern (page 126). This block can also be made using a rotary cutter and ruler.

From dark blue fabric, cut:

• 2 squares 3⅞″ × 3⅞″ or 4 triangles using pattern A

From blue print fabric, cut:

• 6 squares 3⅞″ × 3⅞″ or 12 triangles using pattern A

From medium blue fabric, cut:

• 6 squares 3⅞″ × 3⅞″ or 12 triangles using pattern A

From light blue fabric, cut:

• 2 squares 3⅞″ × 3⅞″ or 4 triangles using pattern A

Newspaper Archive

Appeared in *The Kansas City Star* on March 20, 1937 (block #495)

An Oklahoma woman says she designed this quilt a year or so ago and named it Depression because she heard so many persons say they had difficulty making ends meet at that time. The pattern was contributed by Mrs. Charles C. Ross of Claremore, Oklahoma.

To Make the Block

1. If you cut squares, draw a line from corner to corner on the diagonal on the reverse side of the lightest fabrics. Place 2 of the print squares atop the 2 dark squares with right sides facing and sew ¼″ on either side of the line. Using your rotary cutter, cut on the line. Open each of the half-square triangle units and press toward the dark fabric.

Place the 2 light squares atop 2 of the medium squares and make half-square triangles, following the instructions above.

Place the remaining print squares atop the remaining medium squares and make half-square triangles, following the instructions above.

If you cut triangles, sew them together to make the following half-square triangle units.

- 4 dark/print
- 8 medium/print
- 4 light/medium

2. Sew the half-square triangle units into rows.

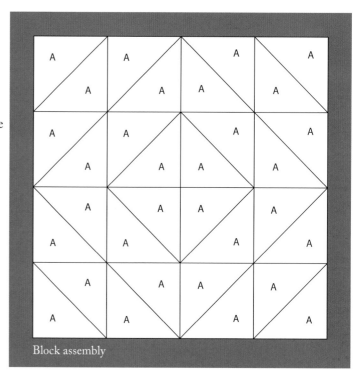

Block assembly

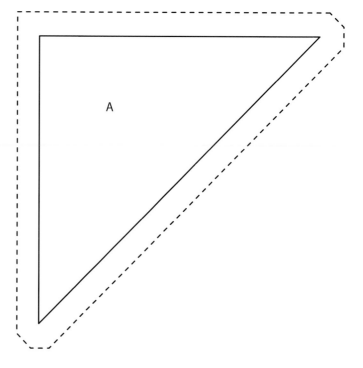

A

3. Sew the rows together to complete the block.

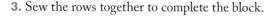

1938 Fair and Square

Finished block: 12″ × 12″

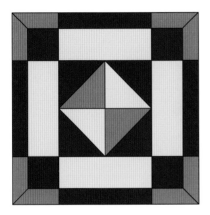

Fabric Needed

Brown • Gold • Orange

Cutting Instructions

Use the Fair and Square patterns (pages 130–131). This block can also be made using a rotary cutter and ruler for the measured pieces.

From brown fabric, cut:

• 4 rectangles 1½″ × 6½″ or use pattern B

• 4 squares 2½″ × 2½″ or use pattern D

• 2 squares 3⅞″ × 3⅞″ or 4 triangles using pattern F

From gold fabric, cut:

• 4 rectangles 2½″ × 6½″ or use pattern E

• 1 square 3⅞″ × 3⅞″ or 2 triangles using pattern F

Newspaper Archive

Appeared in *The Kansas City Star* on March 19, 1938 (block #540)

A quilt block designed from a printed handkerchief. All blocks are made with the same prevailing colors. Blue used all through the quilt of the same shade makes a 12½″ block and takes 21 blocks to make a quilt.

From orange fabric, cut:

• 1 square 3⅞″ × 3⅞″ or 2 triangles using pattern F

• 4 pieces using pattern A

• 4 pieces using pattern C

To Make the Block

If you cut squares from the brown and gold or orange fabrics, draw a line from corner to corner on the diagonal on the reverse side of the lightest colored fabric. Place a light square atop a brown square with right sides facing and sew ¼″ on either side of the line. Using your rotary cutter, cut on the line. Open each of the half-square triangle units and press toward the dark fabric.

If you chose to cut the triangles using pattern F, sew a brown triangle to an orange triangle. Make 2 half-square triangles. Then make 2 more by sewing a brown triangle to a gold triangle. Make 2. You should have a total of 4 half-square triangles.

Sew the half-square triangles together to make the center of the block.

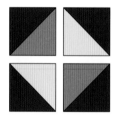

2. Now sew a brown square to either end of a gold rectangle. Make 2.

3. Sew a gold rectangle to either side of the center square.

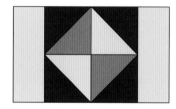

4. Sew the 3 rows together.

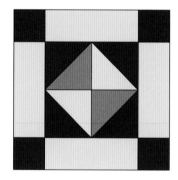

5. Sew an orange A and C piece to either end of a brown B rectangle. The mitered edges of the A and C pieces should always angle toward the outside of the block. Make 4. The orange A and C pieces are to be inset.

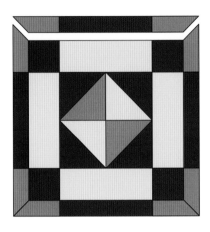

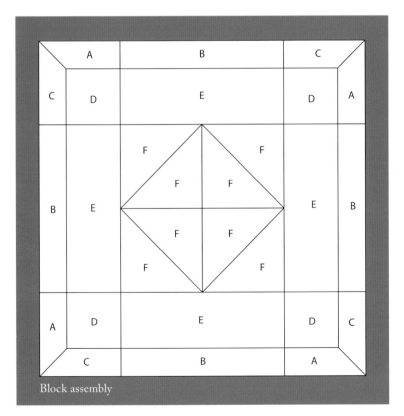

Block assembly

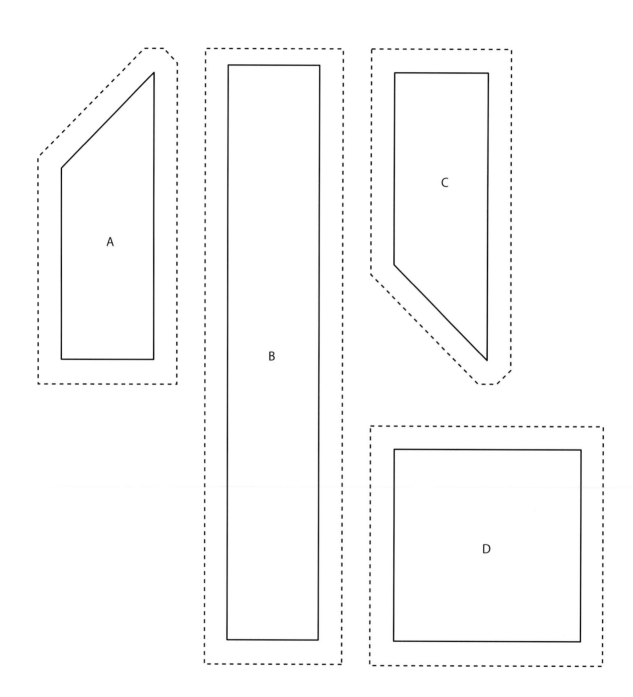

A

B

C

D

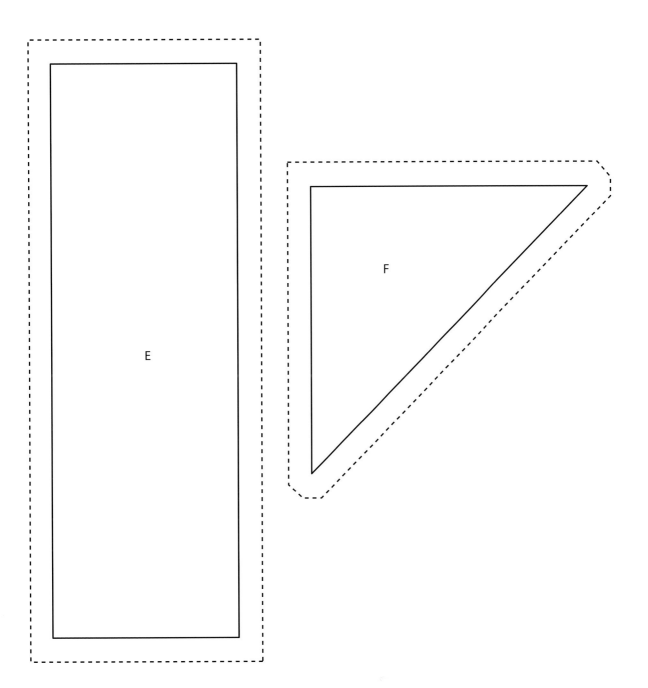

1939 Hexagon Beauty

Finished block: 12″ × 12″

Fabric Needed

Red • Cream

Cutting Instructions

Use the Hexagon Beauty patterns (page 134).

NOTE: The finished measurement for the width is obtained by measuring from point to point. For a true 12″ × 12″ block, add triangles and strips to the hexagon or appliqué it to a 12½″ × 12½″ square.

From red fabric, cut:

- 3 pieces using pattern A
- 3 pieces using pattern B

From cream fabric, cut:

- 3 pieces using pattern A
- 3 pieces using pattern B

Newspaper Archive

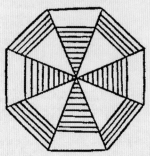

Appeared as an octagon in *The Kansas City Star* on June 14, 1939 (block #581)

Original size: 10″. This pattern is contributed by Miss Alta M. House of Manchester, Kansas.

To Make the Block

1. Sew a red A piece to a cream B piece. Make 3.

2. Sew a cream A piece to a red B piece. Make 3.

3. Sew 3 wedges together, alternating the colors. Make 2.

4. Sew the 2 sections together to complete the block.

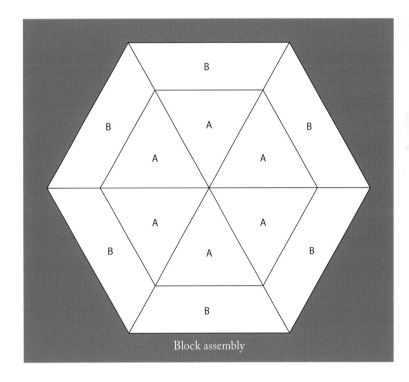

Block assembly

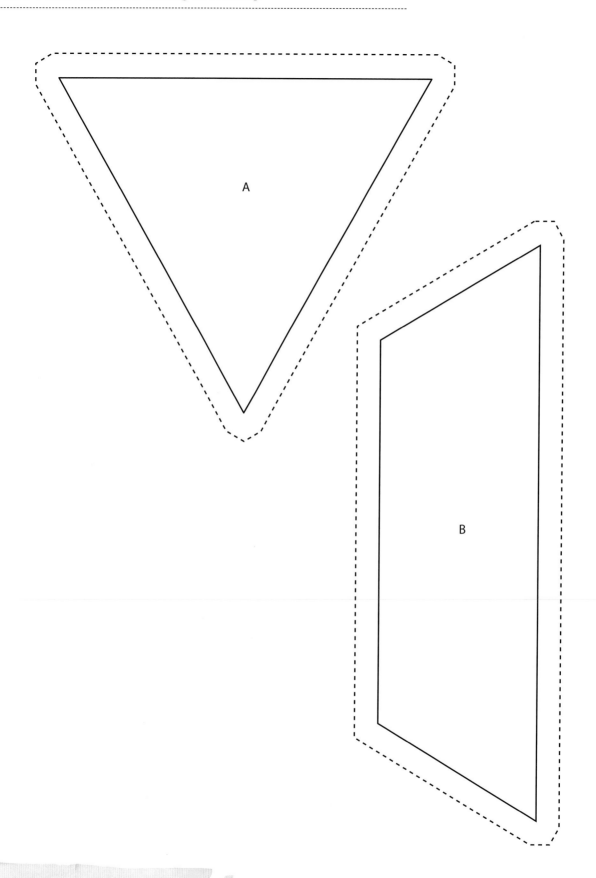

A

B

1940s

See the Little Boy's Britches block (page 182).
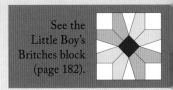

Plaid Britches, owned by Deb Rowden of Lawrence, Kansas; designer unknown; quilted by Lori Kukuk of McLouth, Kansas

1940 Garden Walk

Finished block: 12″ × 12″

Fabric Needed

Dark green • Rose • Cream

Cutting Instructions

Use the Garden Walk patterns (pages 138–139). This block can also be made using a rotary cutter and ruler for the measured pieces.

From dark green fabric, cut:

• 4 triangles using pattern C

• 4 triangles using pattern D

From cream fabric, cut:

• 1 strip 26″ × 2½″ or cut 10 squares
  2½″ × 2½″ (pattern A)

• 4 triangles using pattern B

From rose fabric, cut:

• 1 strip 26″ × 2½″ or cut 10 squares
  2½″ × 2½″ (pattern A)

To Make the Block

1. If you cut 2½″ squares from the cream and rose fabrics, sew them together into four-patch units. If you cut the strips, sew them together horizontally, then cut the strip into 2½″ increments. Make 5 four-patch units.

2. Sew a green D triangle and a green C triangle to either side of a cream B triangle. Make 4.

3. Sew the four-patch units and the triangle units together into rows.

Sew the rows together to complete the block

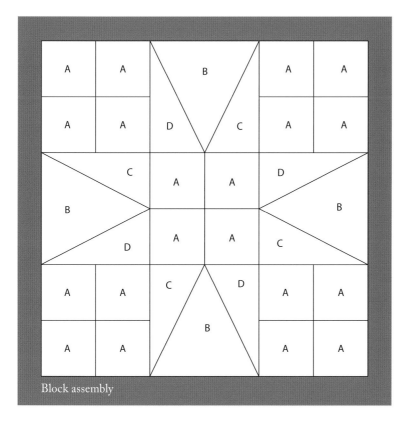

Block assembly

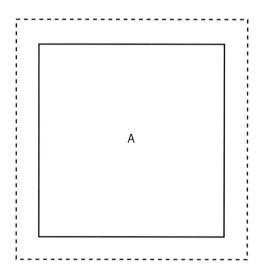

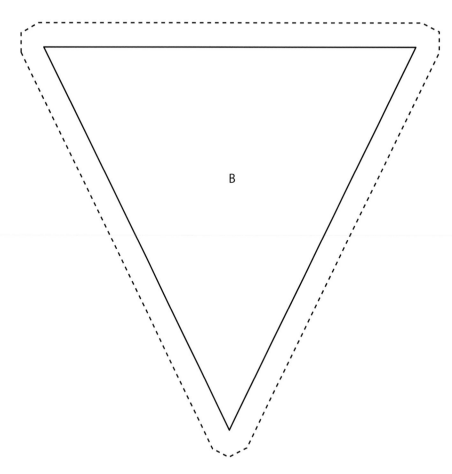

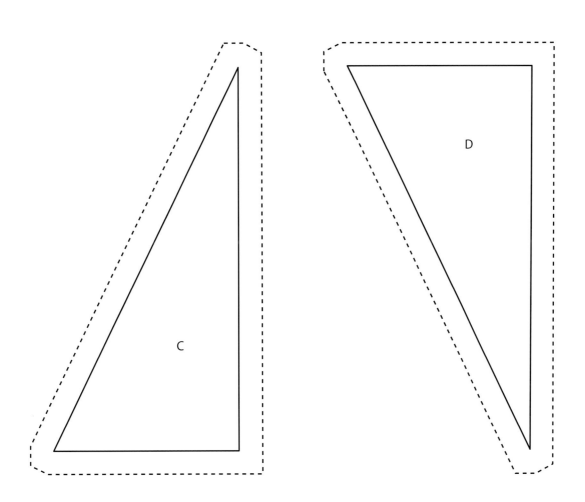

C

D

1940 Comfort Quilt

Finished block: 9″ × 9″

Fabric Needed

Navy blue print • Blue and white shirting

Cutting Instructions

Use the Comfort Quilt patterns (page 142). This block can also be made using a rotary cutter and ruler.

From shirting fabric, cut:

• 8 squares 2½″ × 2½″ or use pattern A

• 1 square 1½″ × 1½″ or use pattern D

From navy blue fabric, cut:

• 4 rectangles 2½″ × 5½″ or use pattern B

• 4 rectangles 1½″ × 2½″ or use pattern C

Newspaper Archive

Appeared in *The Kansas City Star* on May 8, 1940 (block #614)

Original size: 11″. Because this design is adapted to either a quilt or comfort top, Mrs. David M. Lintner of Warwick, Iowa, has named it The Comfort Quilt. One of her comfort tops in this pattern is made with the one-tone pieces in rich purple, the other a print in which purple and gold are the predominating colors.

To Make the Block

1. Begin with the center of the block. Sew a 2½″ A square to either side of a navy blue C rectangle. Make 2.

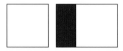

2. Sew a navy blue rectangle to either side of the 1½″ D shirting square.

3. Sew the 3 rows together.

4. Sew a navy blue B rectangle to either side of the center of the block

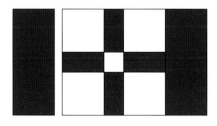

5. Sew a 2½″ A square to either end of a navy blue B rectangle. Make 2. Sew one to the top of the block and one to the bottom.

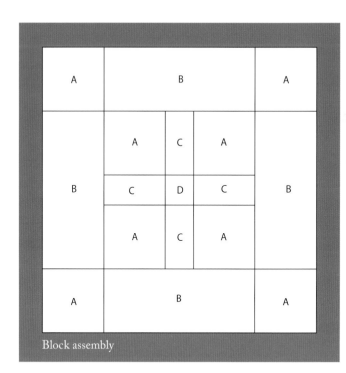

Block assembly

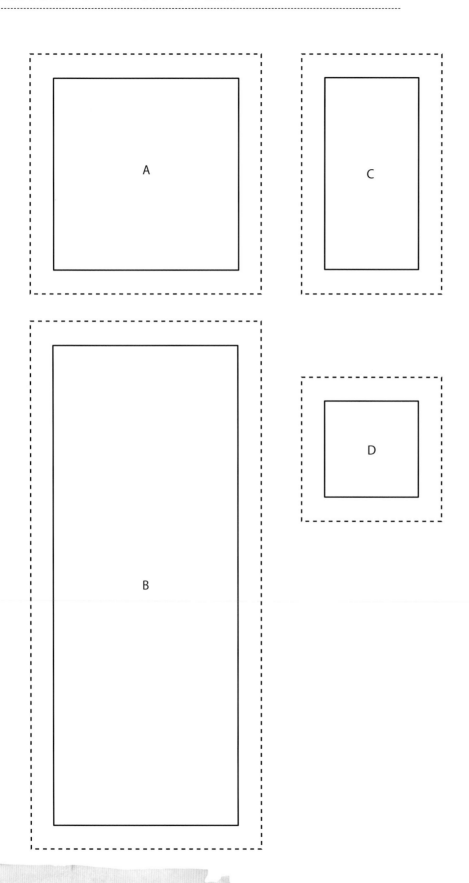

1940 Quilter's Fan

Finished block: 12″ × 12″

Fabric Needed

Cream • Salmon or scraps of your choice

Cutting Instructions

Use the Quilter's Fan pattern (page 144).

From cream fabric, cut:

• 32 pieces using pattern A

From salmon fabric, cut:

• 32 pieces using pattern A

Newspaper Archive

Appeared in *The Kansas City Star* on August 28, 1940 (block #625)

Original size: 5″. We suspect the creator of this design picked up a mental suggestion from the swirling blades of an electric fan. The pattern comes from Mrs. S. E. Axtell of Westphalia, Kansas.

To Make the Block

1. Sew a cream A piece to a salmon A piece. Make 32 pairs.

2. Sew 2 pairs together to make 1 unit.

3. Sew 4 units together to make a row. Make 4.

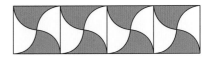

4. Sew the 4 rows together to complete the block.

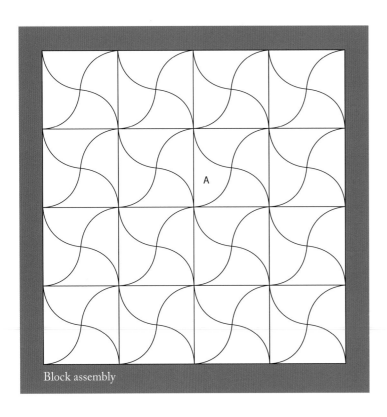

Block assembly

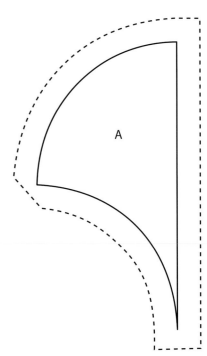

1941 Fence Row

Finished block: 9″ × 9″

Fabric Needed

Dark • Light

Cutting Instructions

Use the Fence Row patterns (page 147). This block can also be made using a rotary cutter and ruler.

NOTE: The original instructions tell you to cut alternating triangles to set the blocks together. It says to cut a square the same size as the unfinished block, then to cut the square once on the diagonal from corner to corner. Use the resulting triangles to "stair step" the blocks into rows. While that may look attractive, you will want to keep in mind that you will be working with bias edges while you are sewing the blocks together. You will also end up with bias edges on the outside of the quilt. Rather than cutting these triangles at 9½″, you would cut them at 9⅞″. If you want to put your quilt together following the original setting, stay stitch the bias edges to cut down on the stretch factor.

Newspaper Archive

Appeared in *The Kansas City Star* on May 21, 1941 (block #648) and previously on April 25, 1931 (block #167)

Original size: 6″. In answer to the many requests for a pattern which uses fancy quilting, we offer our readers this charming old Fence Row design. Any small pattern may be used for the block, the one above showing how effective even such a simple one can be when set together in this way. This is the secret of the charm of this pattern. This block is a nice size, being only 6″ square. Cut plain blocks the same size and then cut these in half (from corner to corner). Set together as shown above, being careful to put the points of the blocks in the exact center of the plain triangles. The blocks do not come directly underneath each other. Mark the design for quilting with a sharp pencil and when quilted the seams will not show. This would be pretty quilted with colored thread if so desired.

From dark fabric, cut:

- 1 square 3½″ × 3½″ or use pattern B
- 2 squares 3⅞″ × 3⅞″ or 4 triangles using pattern A

From light fabric, cut:

- 4 squares 3½″ × 3½″ or use pattern B
- 2 squares 3⅞″ × 3⅞″ or 4 triangles using pattern A

To Make the Block

1. You will need to make 4 half-square triangle units. On the reverse side of the light 3⅞″ squares, draw a line from corner to corner on the diagonal. Place a light square atop a dark square and sew ¼″ on both sides of the line. Cut along the line using your rotary cutter. Open each unit and press toward the darker fabric. If you cut your triangles using the pattern, sew the dark and light A triangles together.

2. Sew the squares and half-square triangles into rows.

3. Sew the rows together to complete the block.

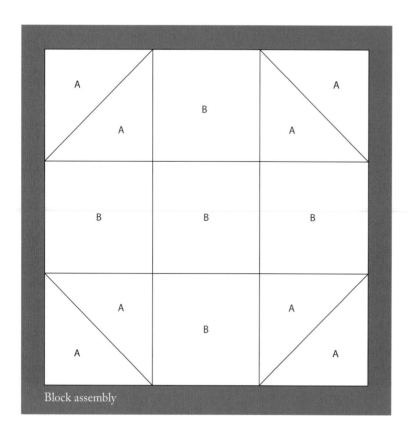

Block assembly

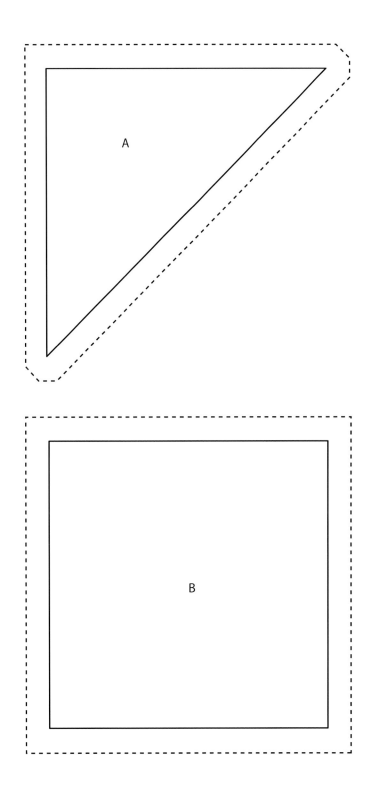

A

B

1941 Star of Alamo

Finished block: 9″ × 9″

Fabric Needed

Brown • Cream (2)

Cutting Instructions

Use the Star of Alamo patterns (pages 149–150).

From brown fabric, cut:

• 4 pieces using pattern D

From one cream fabric, cut:

• 4 pieces using pattern A

From other cream fabric, cut:

• 4 pieces using pattern B

• 1 square using pattern C

Newspaper Archive

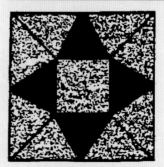

Appeared in *The Kansas City Star* on November 12, 1941 (block #666)

Original size: 8¼″. A youthful, masculine artist contributed this quilt block pattern. He is E. P. Long, Jr., of Bonnerdale, Arkansas, who named the design in honor of his school.

To Make the Block

1. Sew a cream A piece to a brown D piece. Add a cream B piece. Make 4.

2. Stitch the A-D-B sections to the center C square. Stitch across the D-C seamline first, then close the seam between the A and B pieces.

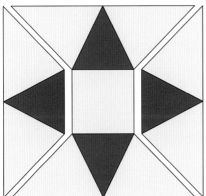

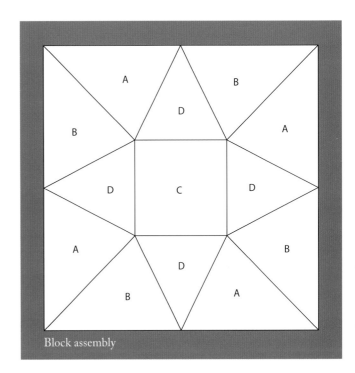

Block assembly

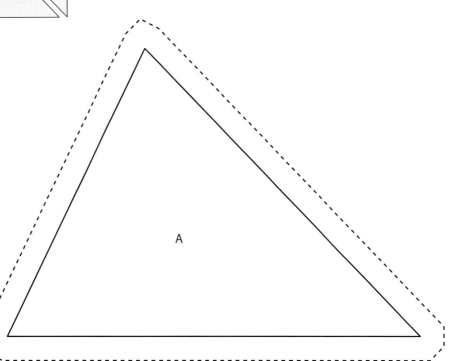

A

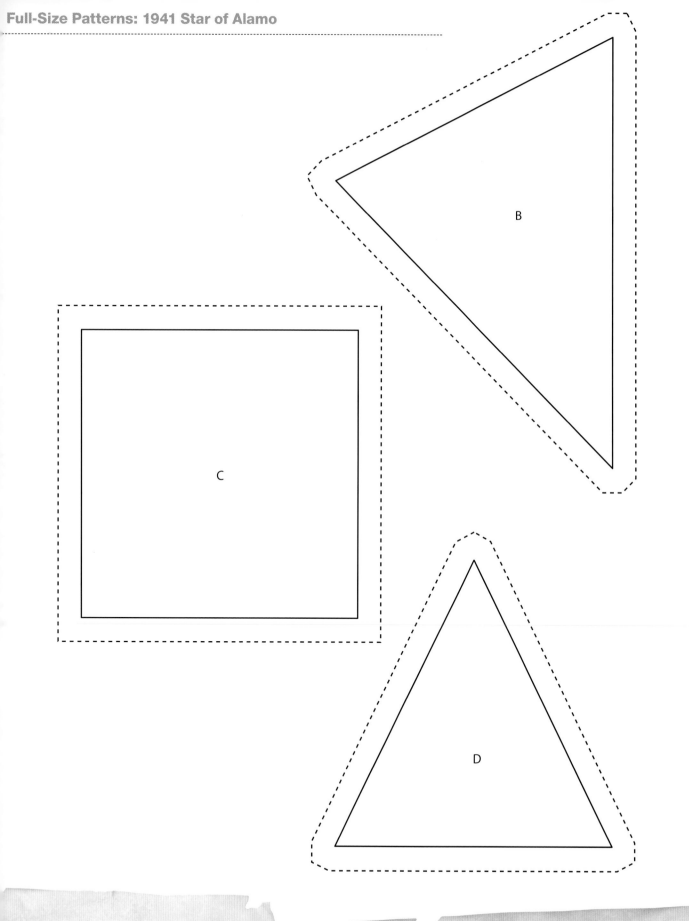

1941 Four-Leaf Clover

Finished block: 10″ × 10″

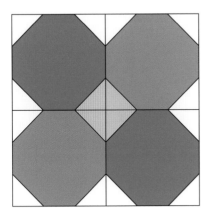

Fabric Needed

Dark greens (2) • Cream • Gold

Cutting Instructions

Use the Four-Leaf Clover patterns (page 153).

From each green fabric, cut:

• 2 octagons using pattern B

From cream fabric, cut:

• 12 triangles using pattern A

From gold fabric, cut:

• 4 triangles using pattern A

Newspaper Archive

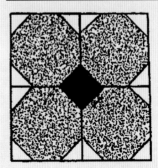

Appeared in *The Kansas City Star* on October 29, 1941 (block #664)

Original size: 9½″. This blocked symbol of good luck departs from its original green and appears with a golden center square surrounded by prints. It is the contribution of Mrs. Harold Purvis of R.R. 1, Franklin, Missouri.

To Make the Block

1. Sew a cream A triangle to 3 corners of a green octagon.

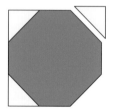

2. Sew a gold A triangle to the remaining octagon corner. This completes 1 quadrant of the block. Make 4.

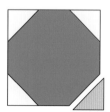

3. Sew the 4 quadrants together to complete the block.

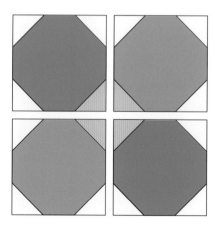

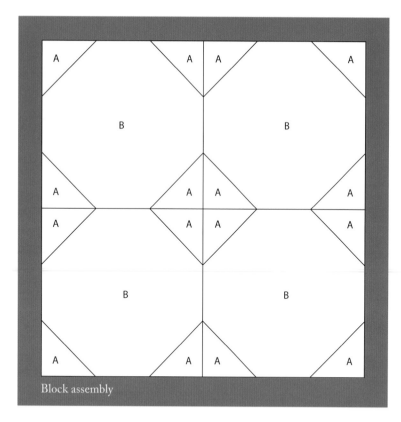

Block assembly

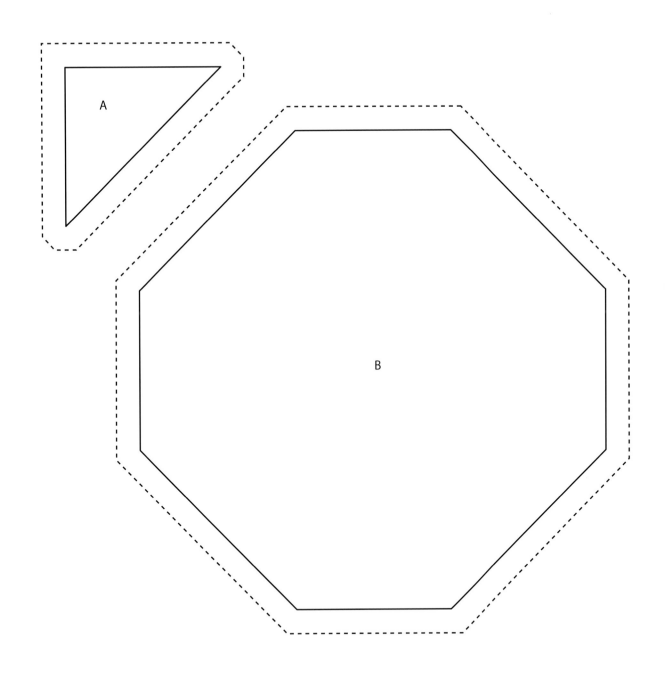

A

B

1941 Radio Windmill

Finished block: 12″ × 12″

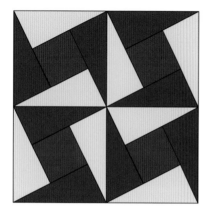

Fabric Needed

Red • Dark blue • Light blue

Cutting Instructions

Use the Radio Windmill patterns (page 156).

NOTE: All A pieces must be cut with the fabric right side up. It cannot be folded.

From red fabric, cut:

• 4 squares using pattern B

From dark blue fabric, cut:

• 8 pieces using pattern A

From light blue fabric, cut:

• 8 pieces using pattern A

Newspaper Archive

Appeared in *The Kansas City Star* on October 22, 1941 (block #663)

Original size: 12¾″. The contributor of this pattern, Miss Anna Killillay of Pleasanton, Iowa, says it may be set with plain blocks or used as an allover pattern. If the latter plan is followed, the quilt will show many small windmills all over the coverlet. For a combination, she suggests a small print and 2 one-tone pieces.

To Make the Block

1. We will use a method called partial seaming to make this block. Partial seaming means that one sews only a portion of one of the seams when beginning to make a block, then goes back and finishes that seam when the rest of the pieces have been sewn in place.

Sew a light blue A piece to the center red square. Only sew halfway to the end of the square and leave the rest of the A piece dangling free. (You'll stitch the rest of this seam last.) The open seam is indicated by a dotted line.

Stop sewing where the dotted line begins.

2. Sew a dark blue A piece in place.

3. Now add a light blue A piece.

4. Sew the dark blue A piece in place.

5. Now go back and close up the first seam. This completes 1 quadrant of the block. Make 4.

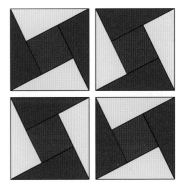

6. Sew the 4 quadrants together to complete the block.

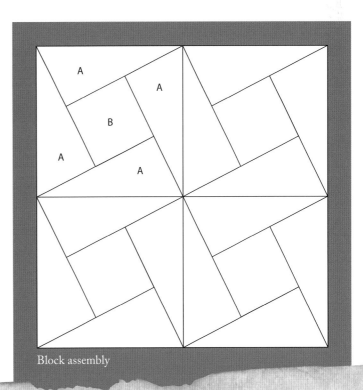

Block assembly

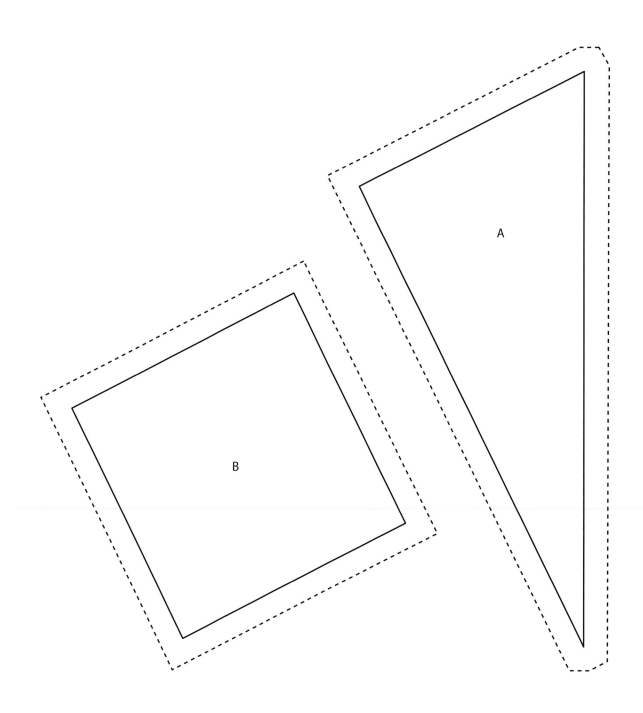

1942 Thorny Thicket

Finished block: 12″ × 12″

Fabric Needed

Tan • Olive green • Dark olive green

Cutting Instructions

Use the Thorny Thicket patterns (page 160).

From tan fabric, cut:

- 8 squares using pattern D
- 4 triangles using pattern A
- 4 triangles using pattern C
- 16 triangles using pattern B

From olive green fabric, cut:

- 16 triangles using pattern B

From dark olive green fabric, cut:

- 8 squares using pattern D
- 4 triangles using pattern E

Newspaper Archive

Appeared in *The Kansas City Star* on August 5, 1942 (block #695)

The much desired Thorny Thicket is supplied by Mrs. Mae Dees of Coldwater, Missouri, who found it among a pattern collection made during her childhood. She says when the youngsters of her day were learning to piece quilts, they were first required to use their small scraps in this pattern before they were permitted to have large new pieces. Sometimes each thorn would be of a different color. Mrs. Dees suggests a color scheme of red, white, and blue. The completed blocks are put together with blue strips 1″ wide, having a white strip of the same width between them, and a red and white nine-patch in the corners.

To Make the Block

1. Alternating the tan and dark olive green squares, sew them together into strips of 4. Make 4 rows and sew the rows together to make the center of the block.

2. Sew the tan and olive green triangles together. Stitch the triangles together into strips of 4. You'll need to make 4 sections like this for the outer part of the block.

3. Now make a corner unit by sewing a tan A and C triangle to the dark green E triangle. Make 4.

4. Sew a corner unit to either end of an outer strip as shown. Make 2.

5. Sew an outer strip to either side of the center square.

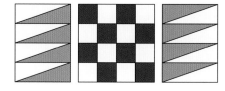

6. Sew the 3 sections together to complete the block.

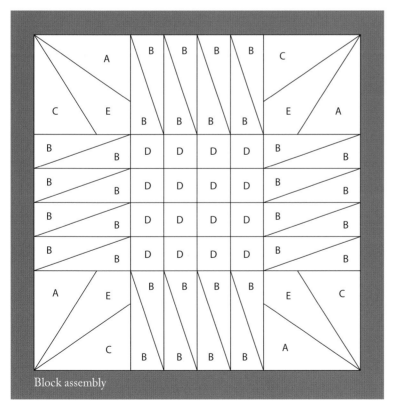

Block assembly

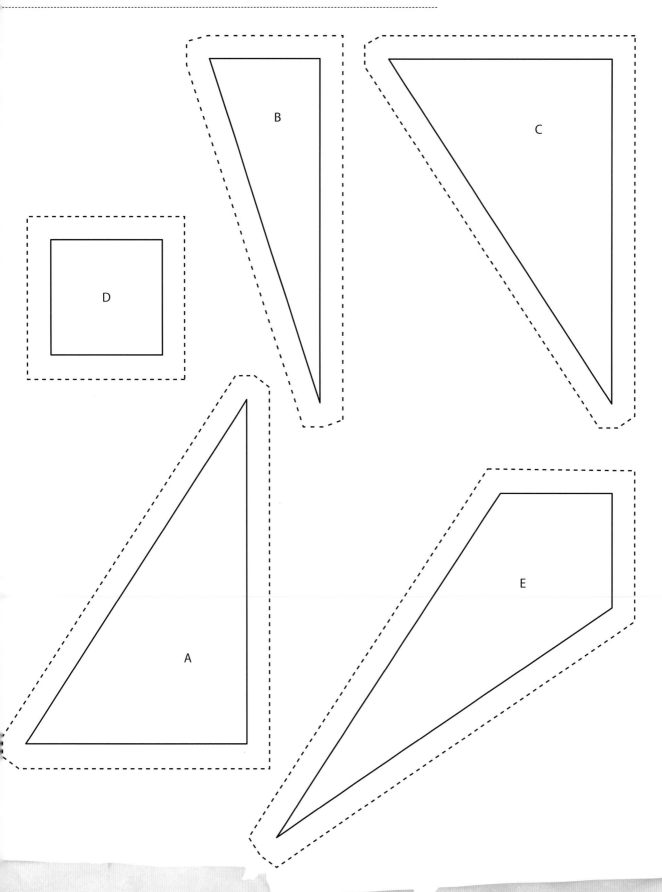

1942 Chain Quilt

Finished block: 12″ × 12″

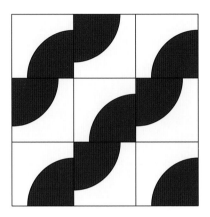

Fabric Needed

Scraps of various shades of blue • Cream

Cutting Instructions

Use the Chain Quilt patterns (page 163).

From cream fabric, cut:

• 9 pieces using pattern A

From blue scraps, cut:

• 9 pieces using pattern B

Newspaper Archive

Appeared in *The Kansas City Star* on February 25, 1942 (block #679)

Original size: 9¾″, pieced. Mrs. A. Matushek of R.R. 3, Cuba, Missouri, contributor of the Chain Quilt pattern, says each row of chains should be worked in one color throughout the quilt. She completed a quilt done in 5 pastel shades: rose, orchid, yellow, pink, and green broadcloth, set in white broadcloth.

To Make the Block

1. Fold each A and each B piece in half and finger-press a crease at the halfway point.

Pin the blue B pieces to the cream A pieces. Begin by matching up the center creases, then match up the ends. Pin the pieces closely around the curve, then stitch in place. Make 9 A-B units per block.

2. Sew the units into rows of 3.

3. Sew the rows together to complete the block.

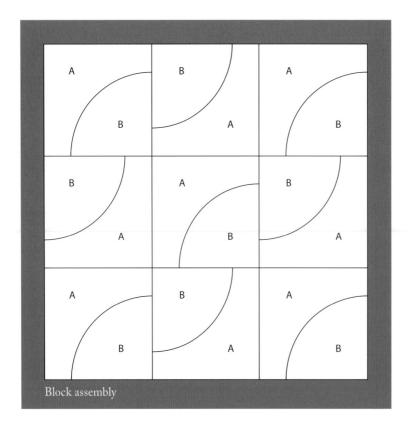

Block assembly

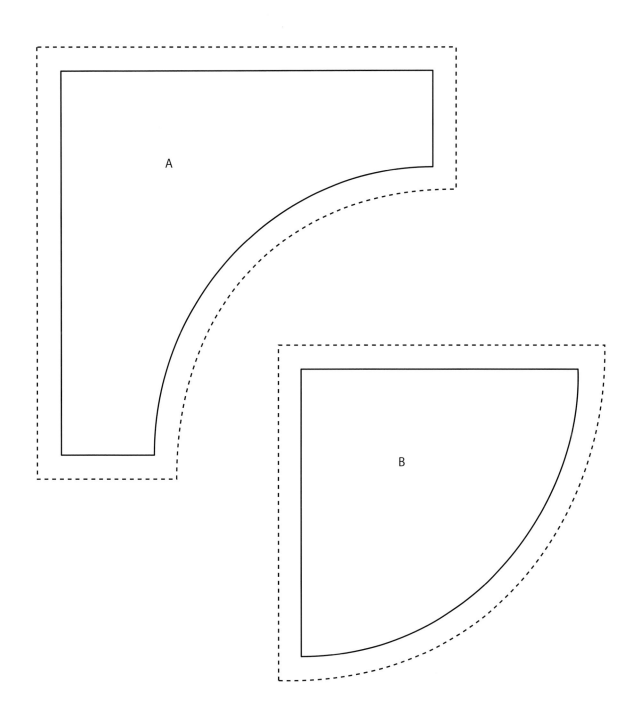

A

B

1942 Rose Bud

Finished block: 12″ × 12″

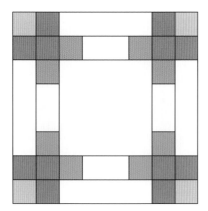

Fabric Needed

Light pink • Dark pink • Green • Cream

Cutting Instructions

Use the Rose Bud patterns (pages 166–167). This block can also be made using a rotary cutter and ruler.

From light pink fabric, cut:

• 4 squares 2″ × 2″ (pattern A)

From dark pink fabric, cut:

• 12 squares 2″ × 2″ (pattern A)

From green fabric, cut:

• 8 squares 2″ × 2″ (pattern A)

From cream fabric, cut:

• 4 rectangles 2″ × 6½″ (pattern B)

• 4 rectangles 2″ × 3½″ (pattern C)

• 1 square 6½″ × 6½″

Newspaper Archive

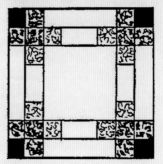

Appeared in *The Kansas City Star* on May 3, 1942 (block #686)

Original size: 12″. This blocked conception of a rosebud is the offering of Eunice P. Turner of Fowler, Kansas. White may be used for the one-tone blocks, but a harmonizing contrast in another color could also be supplied with pleasing effect.

To Make the Block

1. Sew 1 light pink 2″ square to 3 dark pink 2″ squares as shown to make a four-patch unit. Make 4.

2. Sew a green 2″ square to either end of a cream C rectangle. Make 4.

3. Sew a cream B rectangle onto each of the green and cream units.

4. Add a four-patch unit to either end of 2 of the rectangle units.

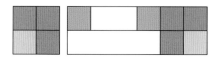

5. Sew a rectangle unit to either side of the center square.

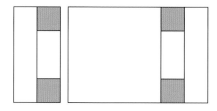

6. Sew the 3 rows together to complete the block.

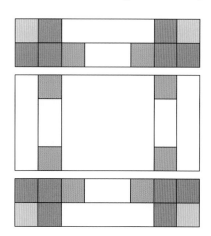

Block assembly

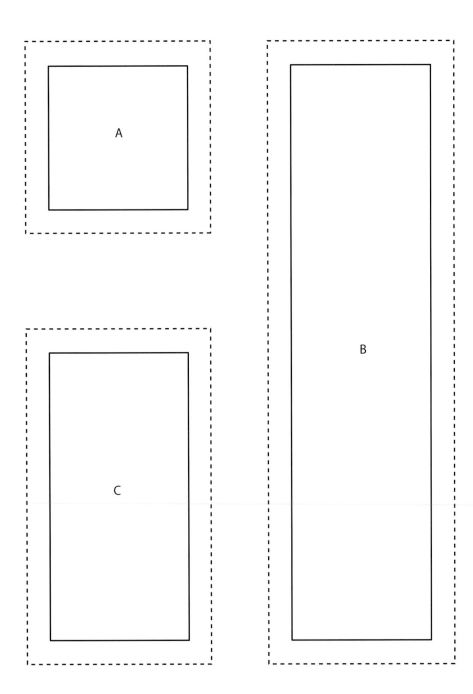

A

B

C

1943 Evelyne's Whirling Dust Storm

Finished block: 12″ × 12″

Fabric Needed

Dark brown print • Light brown print • Tan

Cutting Instructions

Use the Evelyne's Whirling Dust Storm patterns (pages 170–171).

From dark brown print, cut:

• 4 pieces using pattern C

• 4 pieces using pattern E

From light brown print, cut:

• 4 pieces using pattern D

• 4 pieces using pattern E

Newspaper Archive

Appeared in *The Kansas City Star* on May 5, 1943 (block #718)

Original size: 14″. Each completed whirl is appliquéd on a white or other one-tone block.

From tan fabric, cut:

• 4 pieces using pattern A

• 4 pieces using pattern B

To Make the Block

1. Sew a tan A piece to a light brown print E piece. Add a dark brown print C piece. Make 4.

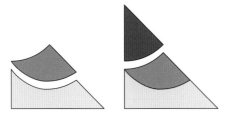

2. Sew a dark brown print E piece to a tan B piece. Add a light brown print D piece. Make 4.

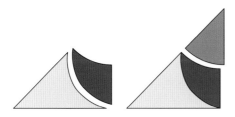

3. Sew the 2 units together. This will complete 1 quadrant of the block. Make 4.

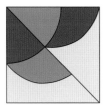

4. Sew the 4 quadrants together to complete the block.

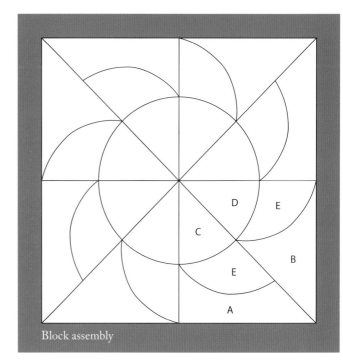

Block assembly

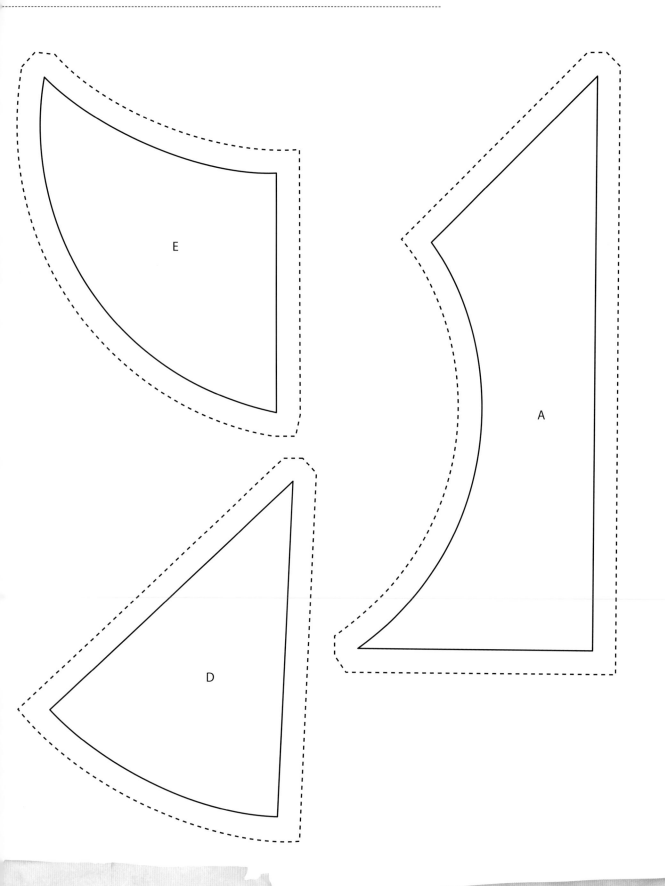

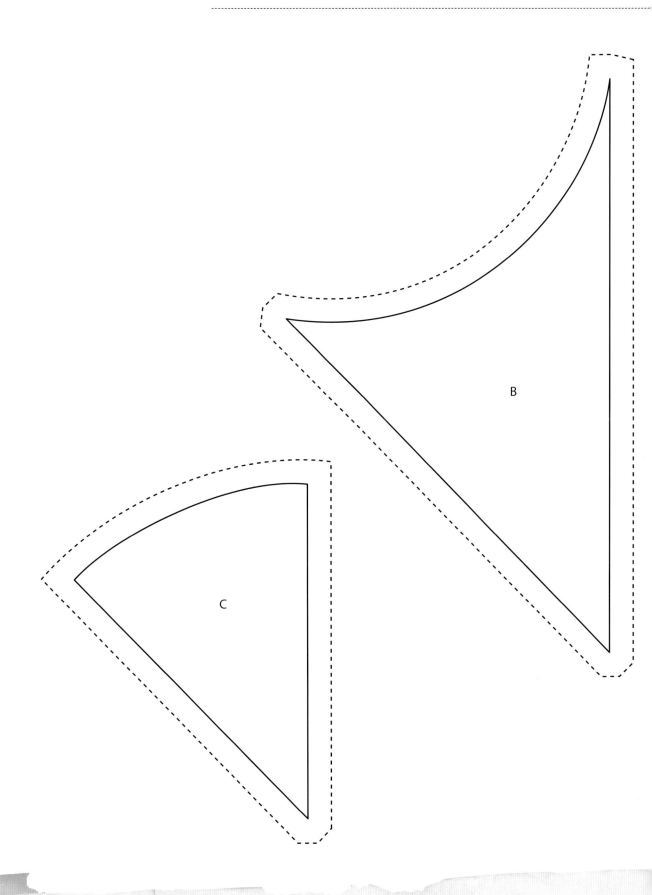

B

C

1944 Friendship Name Chain

Finished block: *6″ × 6″*

Fabric Needed

Red • Black print • Black-and-white shirting
Light tan plaid

Cutting Instructions

Use the Friendship Name Chain patterns (page 174).

From red, cut:

• 4 triangles using pattern B

From black print, cut:

• 1 square 3⅛″ × 3⅛″ (or 2 triangles using pattern B)

From black-and-white shirting, cut:

• 1 square 3⅛″ × 3⅛″ (or 2 triangles using pattern B)

From light tan plaid, cut:

• 1 piece using pattern A

Newspaper Archive

Appeared in *The Kansas City Star* on April 5, 1944 (block #742)

A much-desired quilt block pattern is the Friendship Name Chain, frequently used by organizations of women ambitious to make money. A small charge is made to each person desiring to have his or her name appear on a block. After the quilt has been completed further gain may be realized by selling it at auction. Mrs. Dollie Veatch of Route 2, Lancaster, Missouri, is the contributor of the pattern.

To Make the Block

1. Draw a line from corner to corner on the diagonal on the reverse side of the 3⅛″ black-and-white shirting square. Place the square atop the black 3⅛″ square with right sides facing. Sew ¼″ on both sides of the drawn line. Use your rotary cutter and cut on the drawn line. Open the unit and press toward the darker fabric. This makes a half-square triangle unit. Each square will yield 2 half-square triangles. You need 2 for this block.

Follow the instructions and construct the block on the diagonal.

Sew a red triangle on either side of the half-square triangle. Make 2 units.

2. Sew the strips made from the triangles onto either side of the tan plaid strip to complete the block.

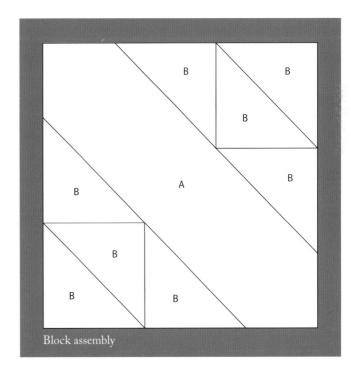

Block assembly

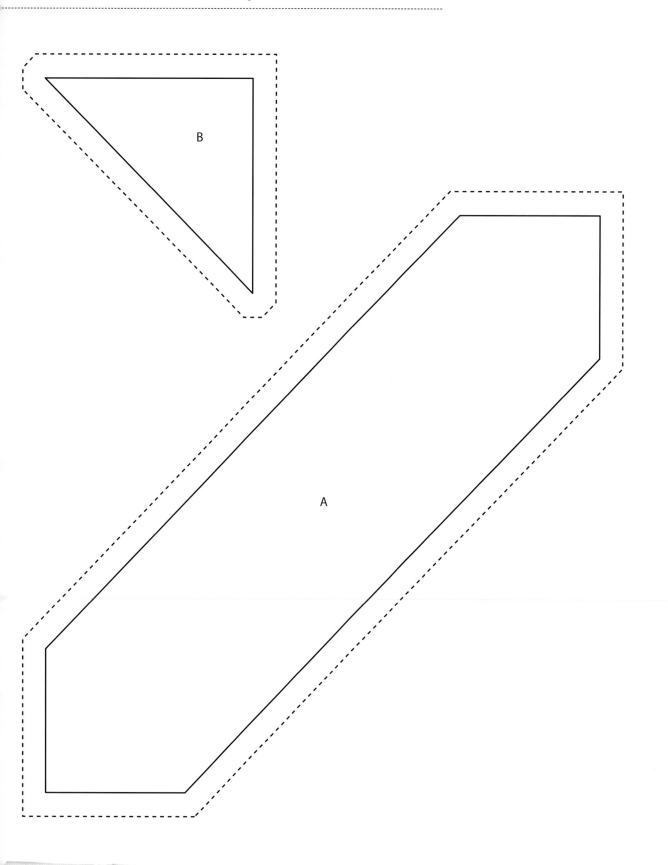

1945 Scottish Cross

Finished block: 12″ × 12″

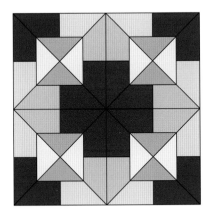

Fabric Needed

Red plaid • Tan plaid • Small plaid
Tan print • Light tan

Cutting Instructions

Use the Scottish Cross patterns (page 178).
This block can also be made using a rotary
cutter and ruler for the measured pieces.

From small plaid fabric, cut:

- 2 squares 4¼″ × 4¼″. Cut the squares from
  corner to corner twice on the diagonal to make
  8 C triangles or use pattern C.

From light tan fabric, cut:

- 2 squares 4¼″ × 4¼″. Cut the squares from
  corner to corner twice on the diagonal to make
  8 C triangles or use pattern C.

Newspaper Archive

Appeared in *The Kansas City Star*
on April 4, 1945 (block #763)

Very effective is this design
in its use of white and dark
one-tone pieces, combined
with plain and print triangles.
Mrs. Chester F. Duncan of
Route 1, Carson, Iowa, is the
designer.

From red plaid fabric, cut:

- 8 pieces using pattern A
- 8 pieces using pattern B

From tan plaid fabric, cut:

- 4 pieces using pattern A
- 4 pieces using pattern B

From tan print fabric, cut:

- 4 pieces using pattern A
- 4 pieces using pattern B

To Make the Block

1. Sew the tan plaid A pieces to the tan plaid B pieces. Make 4.

2. Sew a red A piece to a red B piece. Make 4.

3. Sew a red plaid A-B unit to a tan plaid A-B unit. Add a light tan C triangle to either side. Make 2.

4. Sew a red plaid A-B unit to a tan plaid A-B unit. Add a small plaid C triangle to either side. Make 2.

5. Sew the 4 units together to make the center of the block.

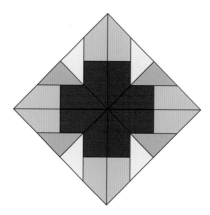

6. Sew the remaining red plaid A and B pieces to the tan A and B pieces. You should have 4 strips.

7. And 4 strips.

8. Add a small plaid triangle to 4 of the strips so you will have 4 A-B-C units.

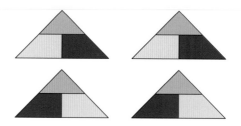

9. Now sew a light tan C triangle to the remaining strips, making 4 A-B-C units.

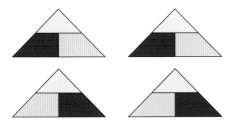

10. Sew the corner units together. Make 4.

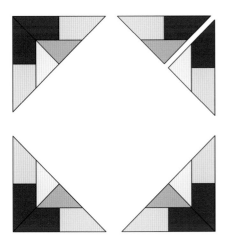

11. Sew the corner units to the center of the block.

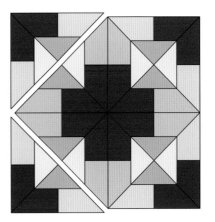

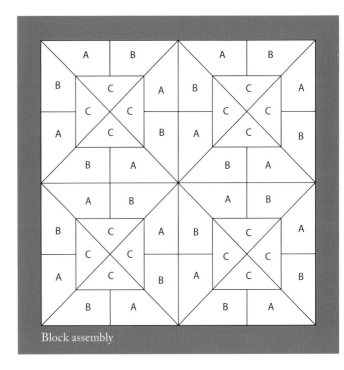

Block assembly

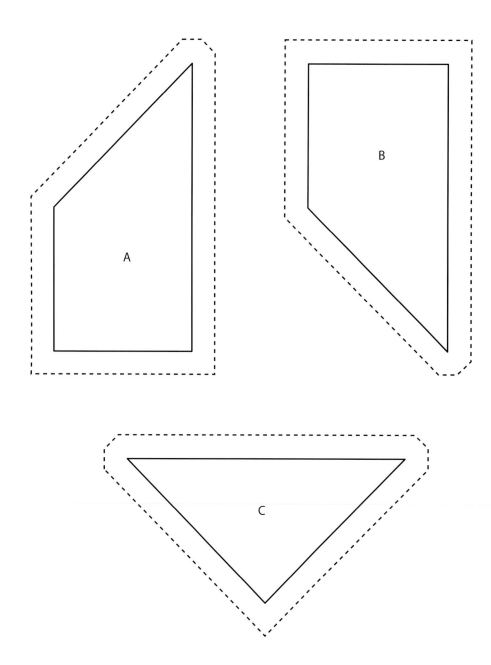

1946 Return of the Swallows

Finished block: 12″ × 12″

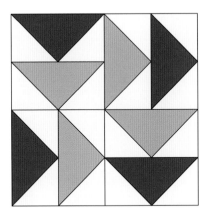

Fabric Needed

Dark blue • Medium blue • Cream

Cutting Instructions

Use the Return of the Swallows patterns (page 181). This block can also be made using a rotary cutter and ruler.

From dark blue fabric, cut:

• 1 square 7¼″ × 7¼″ or 4 triangles using pattern A. Cut the square from corner to corner twice on the diagonal.

From medium blue fabric, cut:

• 1 square 7¼″ × 7¼″ or 4 triangles using pattern A. Cut the square from corner to corner twice on the diagonal.

Newspaper Archive

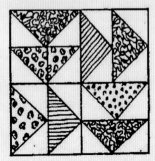

Appeared in *The Kansas City Star* on October 2, 1946 (block #796)

This is one of the popular quilt blocks designed by Mrs. A. B. Snyder of Flats, Nebraska. All the triangular pieces are the same. The center of the quilt is the square of triangles. Increase in size is achieved by adding strips of plain and print triangles with white strips of material set between.

From cream fabric, cut:

• 8 squares 3⅞″ × 3⅞″ or 16 triangles using pattern B. Cut the squares from corner to corner once on the diagonal.

To Make the Block

1. Sew 2 of the cream
B triangles to a medium blue
A triangle. Make 4.

2. Sew the remaining cream
B triangles to the dark blue
A triangles. Make 4.

3. Sew the Flying Geese
together. Notice the change in
position where you stitch the
dark blue Flying Geese.

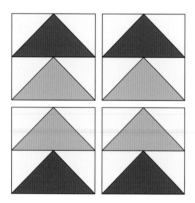

4. Sew the units together to complete the block.

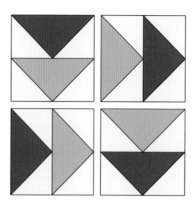

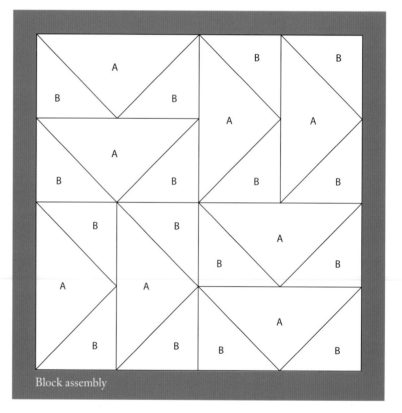

Block assembly

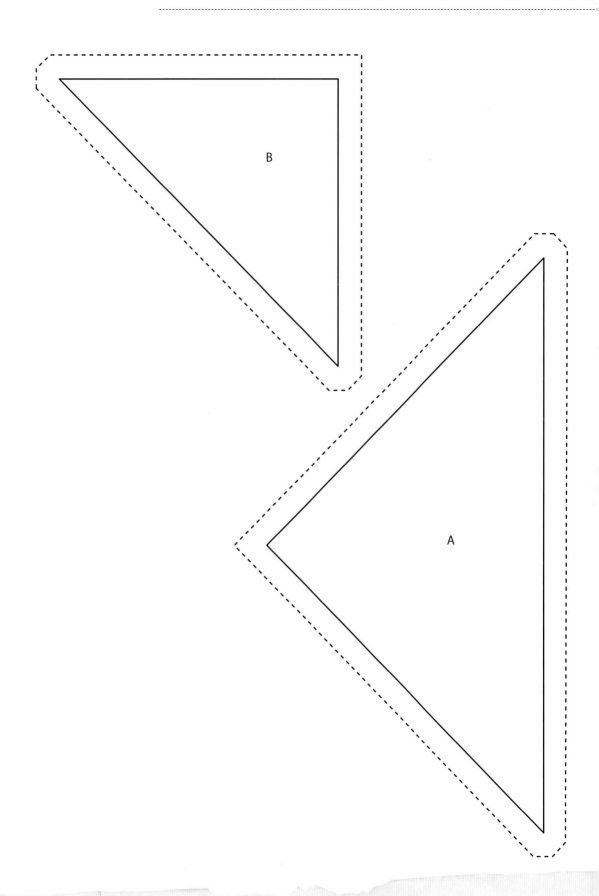

1947 Little Boy's Britches

Finished block: 12″ × 12″

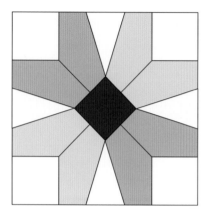

Fabric Needed

Cream shirting for background
Medium blue (denim color)
Light blue (chambray color)
Dark blue

Cutting Instructions

Use the Little Boy's Britches patterns (pages 184–185).

From shirting fabric, cut:

- 4 squares using pattern A
- 4 triangles using pattern C

From medium blue fabric, cut:

- 2 pieces using pattern D
- 2 pieces using pattern B

From light blue fabric, cut:

- 2 pieces using pattern D
- 2 pieces using pattern B

From dark blue fabric, cut:

- 1 square using pattern E

Newspaper Archive

Appeared in *The Kansas City Star* on April 23, 1947 (block #799) and previously September 6, 1939 (block #590). It also ran three times as Little Boy's Breeches on March 31, 1934 (block #347), July 16, 1938 (block #554), and May 17, 1961 (block #1061).

Original size: 9″, pieced.

As Little Boy's Britches:

From 1947: This is a pattern in which both piecing and setting together of individual blocks are easily accomplished. The key to pleasing effectiveness is to alternate dark with light pieces, with the dark being preferably print and the light in one tone

From 1939: Aside from the fact that this pattern is a relatively easy one to put together, it is a design in which print and one-tone materials are effectively combined. The pattern was sent to *The Weekly Star* by Miss Hazel Brinley of Hillsboro, Missouri.

As Little Boy's Breeches:

From 1934: The Little Boy's Breeches quilt pattern is a native Missourian, having been contributed to *The Star* by Mrs. J. H. Tine of Chaonia, Missouri. The dark pieces and light pieces are combined in an interesting wheel arrangement. Allow for seams.

From 1938: Here is an old pattern which has taken on new lines and an engaging new name, Little Boy's Breeches, from the design, which may be in blue on white.

From 1961: For any boy's room, this quilt of pieced Little Boy's Breeches would be very appropriate. The simple design comes from Mrs. Frank Stuever of Wichita, Kansas.

To Make the Block

1. Sew the medium blue B and D pieces together.

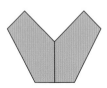

2. Inset the A square.

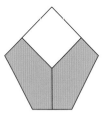

3. Add a C triangle to either side. Make 2 units.

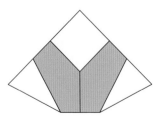

4. Stitch the light blue B and D pieces together.

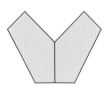

5. Inset the A square. Make 2.

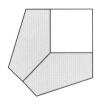

6. Sew the light blue units to the center square.

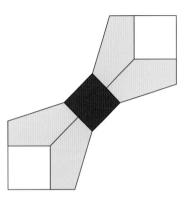

7. Inset the A square. Make 2.

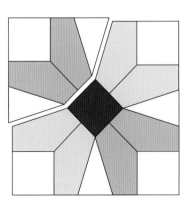

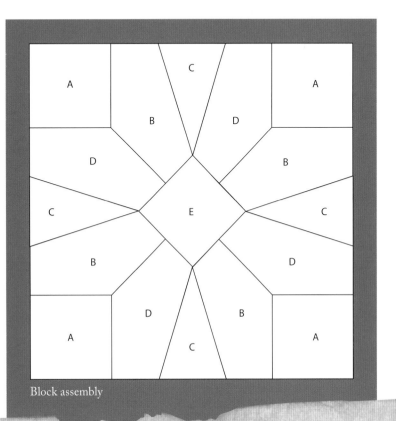

Block assembly

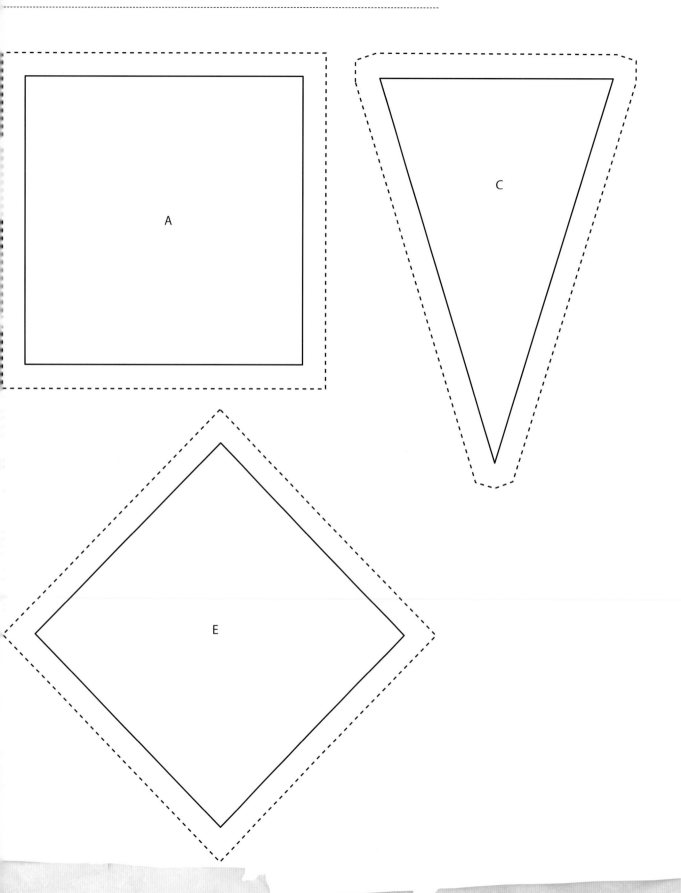

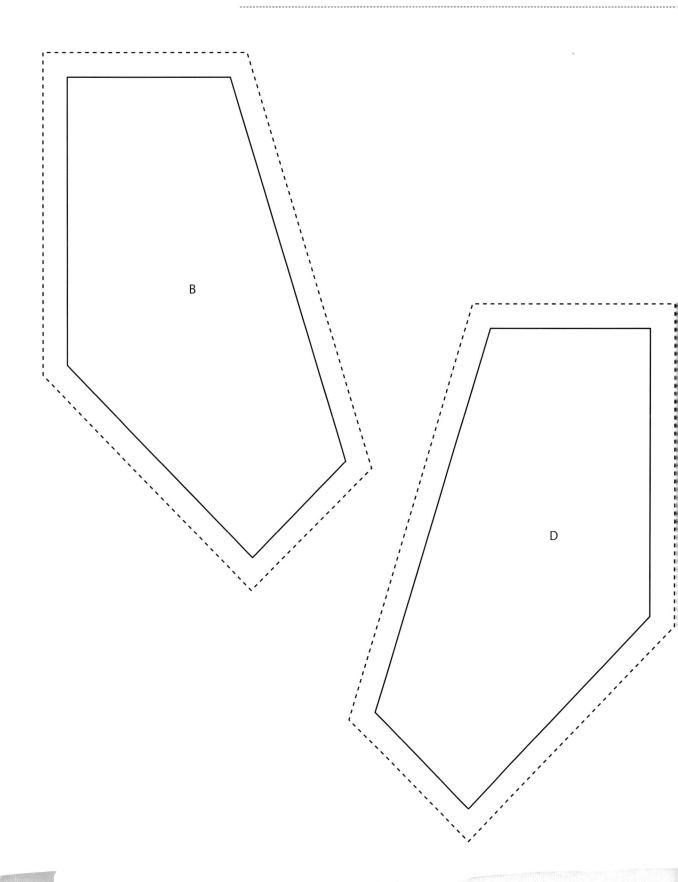

1948 Granny's Choice

Finished block: 12″ × 12″

Fabric Needed

Red print • White print

Cutting Instructions

Use the Granny's Choice patterns (pages 188–189).

From red print fabric, cut:

- 2 pieces using pattern A
- 2 pieces using pattern B
- 2 pieces using pattern C

From white print fabric, cut:

- 2 pieces using pattern A
- 2 pieces using pattern B
- 2 pieces using pattern C

Newspaper Archive

Appeared in *The Kansas City Star* on December 29, 1948 (block #843)

Original size: 6″. Inspiration for this pieced quilt was gained by Mrs. Lonzo E. Cox of Route 2, Thayer, Missouri, from an old hand-woven New England coverlet.

To Make the Block

1. Sew a red print C square to a white print B piece. Make 2.

2. Sew a white print C square to a red print B piece. Make 2.

3. Sew the B/C pieces to the A triangles. The white print B pieces are paired with the white print A triangles. The red print B pieces are paired with the red A triangles.

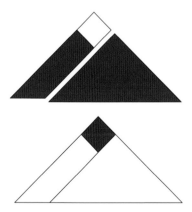

4. Sew the block together.

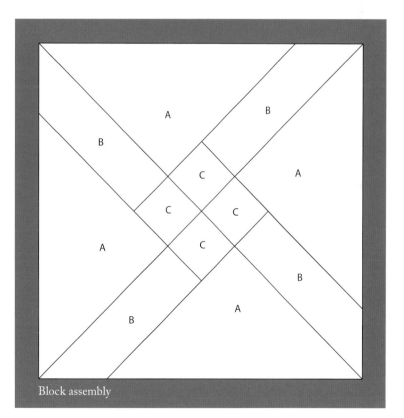

Block assembly

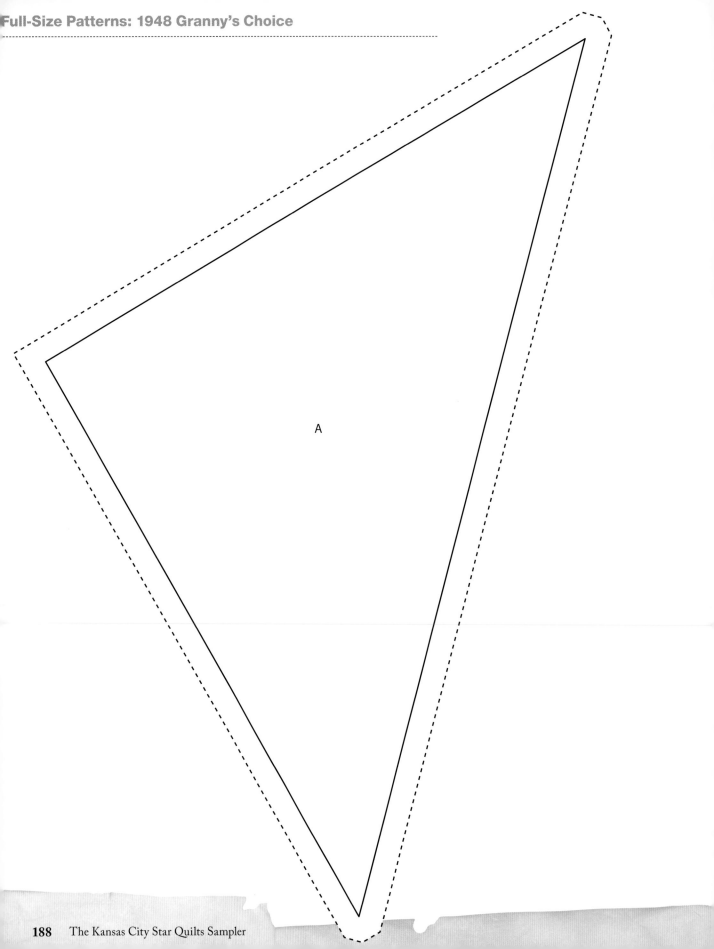

A

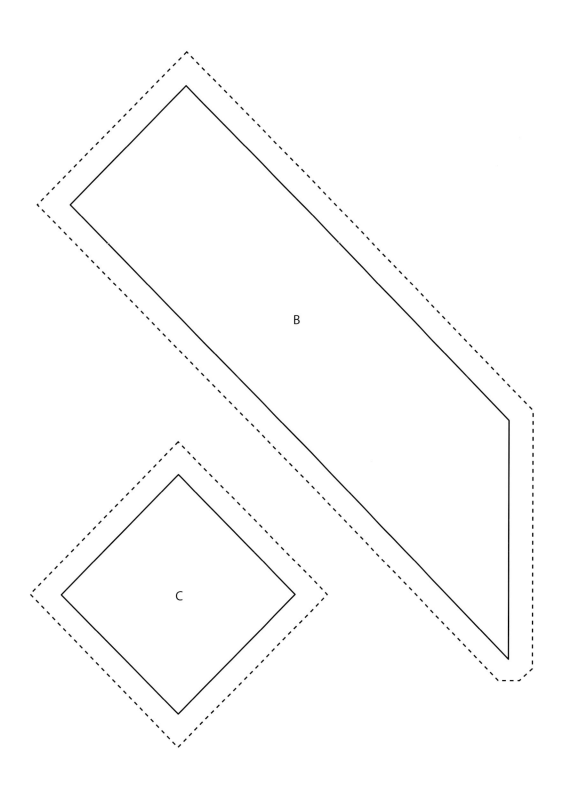

B

C

1949 Crazy Anne #2

Finished block: 12″ × 12″

Fabric Needed

Dark green • Red
Red, green, and white background print

Cutting Instructions

Use the Crazy Anne #2 patterns (pages 192–194).

From red fabric, cut:

- 4 triangles using pattern H
- 4 pieces using pattern E

From green fabric, cut:

- 4 triangles using pattern G
- 4 pieces using pattern B

Newspaper Archive

Appeared in *The Kansas City Star* on June 15, 1949 (block #264)

Very distinctive is this quilt block with its whorl of prints accented by one-tone pieces.

From background print, cut:

- 4 pieces using pattern D
- 4 pieces using pattern C
- 4 pieces using pattern A
- 4 pieces using pattern F

To Make the Block

1. Sew a dark green G triangle to a background D piece. Add the red E piece, then the background F triangle. Make 4 of these units.

2. Sew a red H triangle to a background C piece. Then add a green B piece. Sew on the A triangle. Make 4 of these units.

3. Sew the units together into pairs to make up one-quarter of the block.

4. Sew the block together.

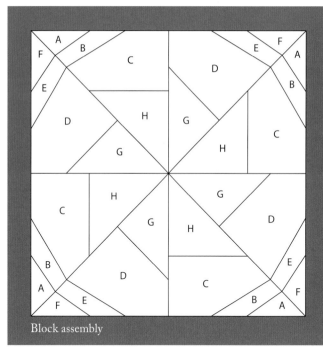

Block assembly

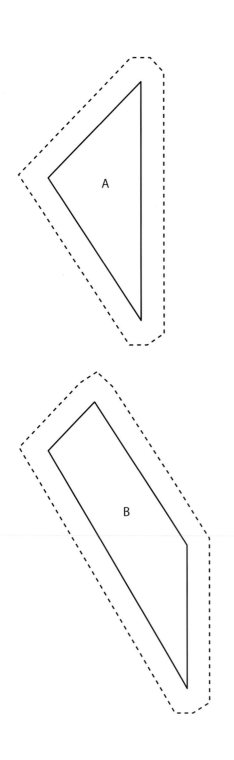

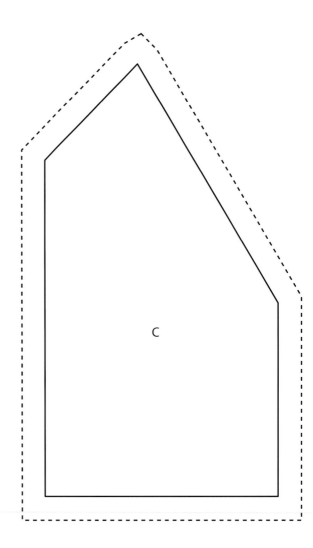

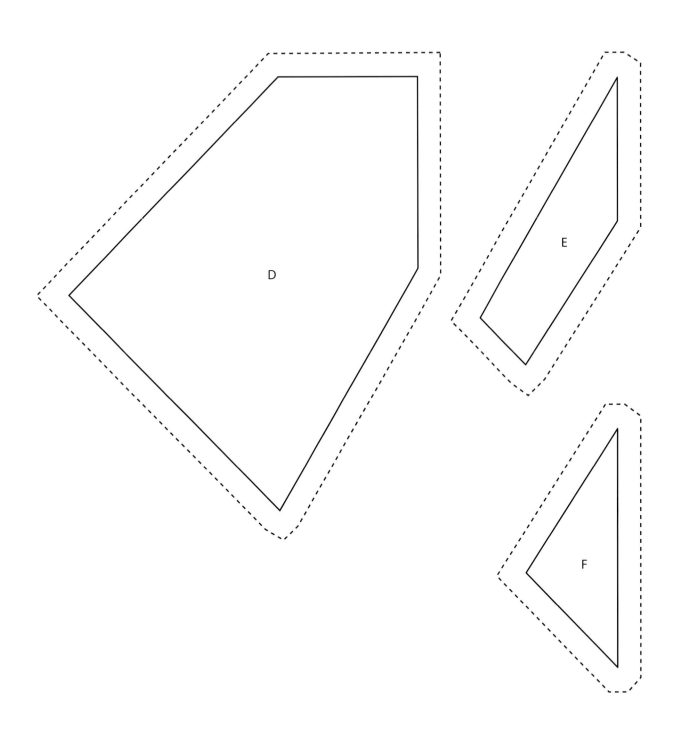

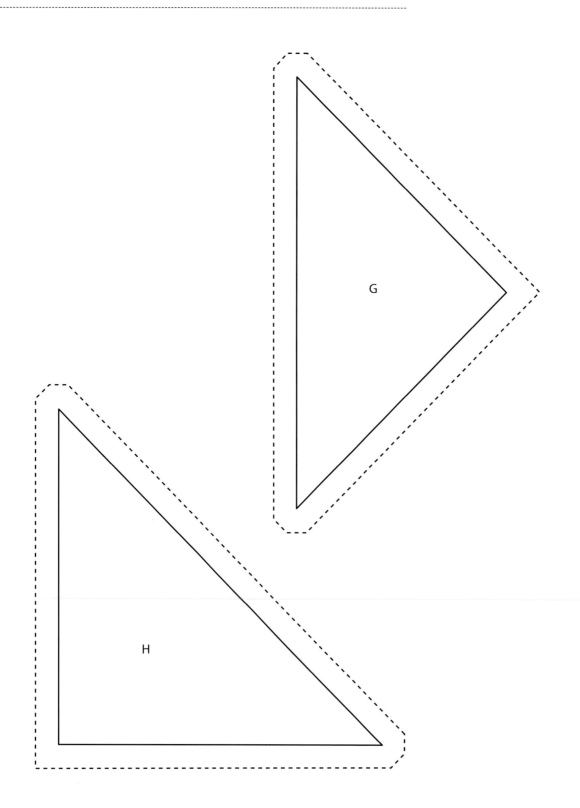

G

H

1950s

See the Rising Sun block (page 231).

Rising Sun, submitted by Sue Bouchard, Vista, California; quiltmaker unknown; owned by Sue Bouchard

1950 Love in a Tangle

Finished block: 12″ × 12″

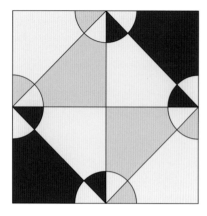

Fabric Needed

Light blue • Dark blue • Tan

Cutting Instructions

Use the Love in a Tangle patterns (page 199).

From tan fabric, cut:

• 4 pieces using pattern A

• 8 pieces using pattern B

From dark blue fabric, cut:

• 2 pieces using pattern A

• 4 pieces using pattern B

From light blue fabric, cut:

• 2 pieces using pattern A

• 4 pieces using pattern B

Newspaper Archive

Appeared in *The Kansas City Star* on February 2, 1950 (block #865)

Original size: 12″. An interesting allover design is Love in a Tangle. The pattern comes from Mrs. Hulbert Austin of Borger, Texas. It was given to her mother about 45 years ago by a woman living near Stillwater, Oklahoma, when that area was a part of Oklahoma Territory, and represents her interpretation of a complicated romance. Mrs. Austin's coverlet is 14 blocks long and 12 blocks wide.

To Make the Block

1. Sew a dark blue B piece to either end of a tan A piece. Make 2 units.

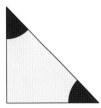

2. Sew a tan B piece to either end of a dark blue A piece. Make 2 units.

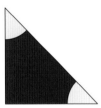

3. Sew the units together. You'll need 2 units.

4. Sew a light blue B piece to either end of a tan A piece. Make 2 units.

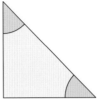

5. Sew a tan B piece to either end of a light blue A piece. Make 2 units.

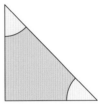

6. Sew the units together. You'll need 2 units.

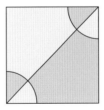

7. Sew the 4 units together to complete the block.

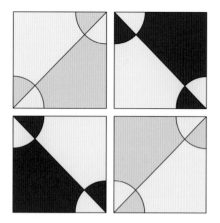

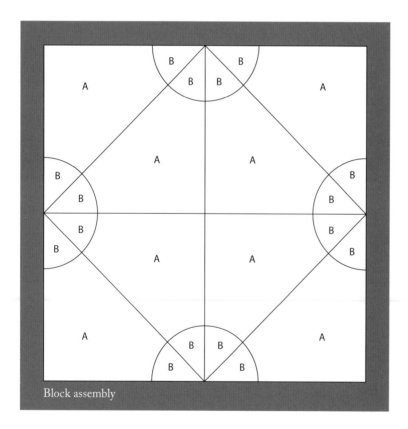

Block assembly

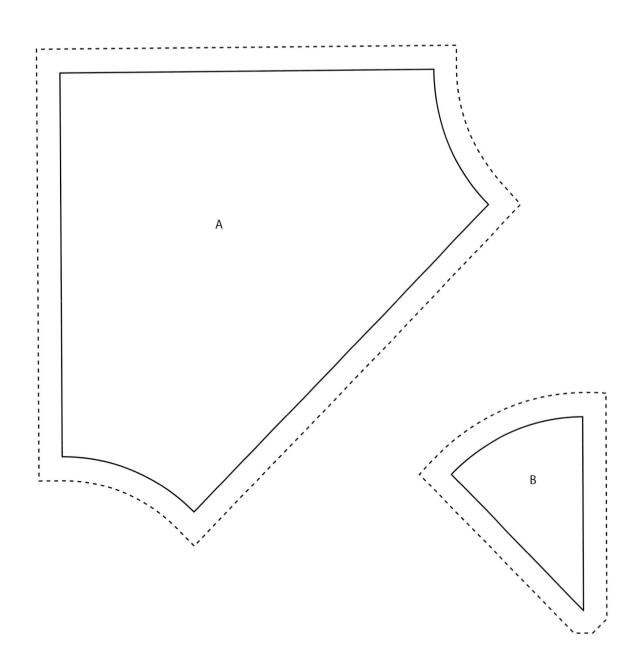

A

B

1950 Queen Charlotte's Crown

Finished block: 12″ × 12″

Fabric Needed

Dark red print • Tone-on-tone dark red
Red and white shirting • White for background

Cutting Instructions

Use the Queen Charlotte's Crown patterns (page 202). This block can also be made using a rotary cutter and ruler.

From white fabric, cut:

• 4 squares 2⅞″ × 2⅞″ (pattern A)

• 6 squares 3¼″ × 3¼″ or 12 triangles using pattern B

From dark red print fabric, cut:

• 3 squares 2⅞″ × 2⅞″ (pattern A)

• 4 squares 3¼″ × 3¼″ or 8 triangles using pattern B

Newspaper Archive

Appeared in *The Kansas City Star* on February 22, 1950 (block #868)

Original size: 6″. Much of the effectiveness of this design is attained by choosing a small print in vivid colors for the triangular quilt blocks and keeping the tips of the blocks sharp. The pattern comes from Mrs. Bertha Troutman of Ottumwa, Iowa.

From tone-on-tone dark red fabric, cut:

• 4 squares 3¼″ × 3¼″ or 8 triangles using pattern B

From shirting fabric, cut:

• 2 squares 2⅞″ × 2⅞″ (pattern A)

• 2 squares 3¼″ × 3¼″ or 4 triangles using pattern B

To Make the Block

Use a scant ¼″ seam allowance when sewing.

1. You will need to make half-square triangle units for this block.

To make half-square triangles, draw a line from corner to corner on the diagonal on the reverse side of the lightest fabric. Place a light square atop a darker square and sew ¼″ on each side of the line. Use your rotary cutter and cut on the line. Open each unit and press toward the darkest fabric.

Make 4 dark red print/background half-square triangles, 8 dark red tone-on-tone/background half-square triangles and 4 shirting/dark red print half-square triangles.

Sew the squares and half-square triangles together into rows. You will need to make 5 rows.

2. Sew the rows together to complete the block.

Press the seam allowances under on the outer edges of each of the leaves and pin in place. The center and point of each leaf should line up with the crease that goes toward each corner. Tuck the widest end of each leaf under the flower. Appliqué all in place.

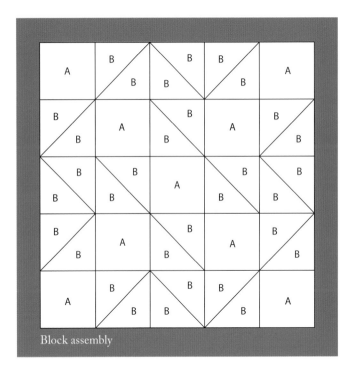

Block assembly

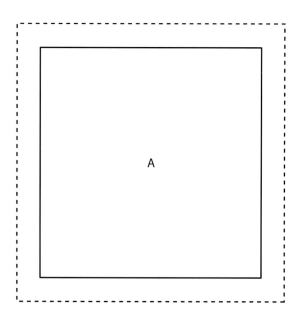

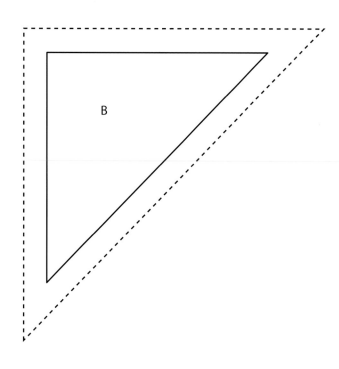

1951 Garden Star

Finished block: 9″ × 9″

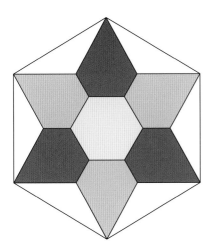

Fabric Needed

Dark lavender • Medium lavender
Yellow • Cream

Cutting Instructions

Use the Garden Star patterns (page 205).

NOTE: The finished measurement for the height is obtained by measuring from point to point. For a true 9″ × 9″ block, add triangles and strips to the hexagon or appliqué it to a 9½″ × 9½″ square.

From dark lavender fabric, cut:

• 3 petals using pattern C

From medium lavender fabric, cut:

• 3 petals using pattern C

From yellow fabric, cut:

• 1 hexagon using pattern A

From cream fabric, cut:

• 6 triangles using pattern B

Newspaper Archive

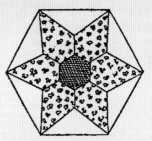

Appeared in *The Kansas City Star* on May 30, 1951 (block #891) and previously on May 8, 1937 (block #502)

From 1951: Original size: 8½″. This is one of several versions of the Flower Garden quilt block. The pointed print blocks are arranged around the one-tone center block as the petals of a flower. A suggestion is to choose for the center block a one-tone fabric and to make the outer triangles in a different shade of this color instead of white as is indicated in the original design.

From 1937: Original size: 8½″. This is a variation of the flower garden design. The hexagonal blocks are extended to a point and arranged around the central block as petals of a flower.

To Make the Block

1. Alternate the dark and medium petals and stitch the flat edge of each petal to the center yellow hexagon.

2. Close the seam between each of the petals.

3. Inset a B triangle between each petal to complete the block.

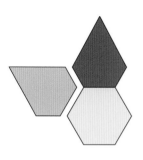

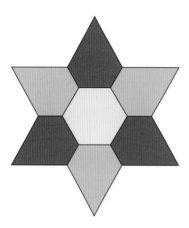

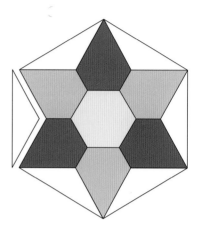

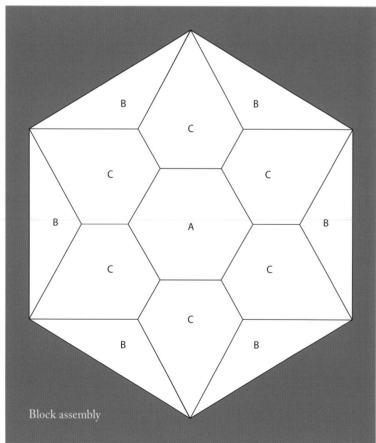

Block assembly

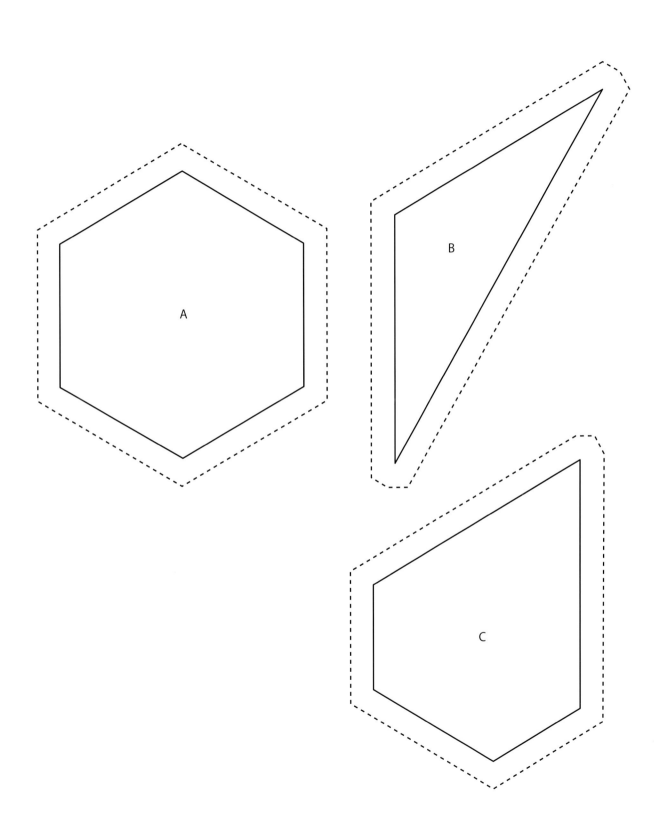

1952 Wagon Wheels Carry Me Home

Finished block: 12″ × 12″

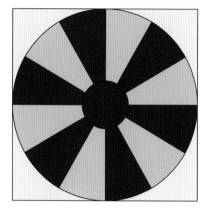

Fabric Needed

Pink • Brown • Tan

Cutting Instructions

Use the Wagon Wheels Carry Me Home patterns (page 208). This block uses a combination of appliqué and piecing.

From pink fabric, cut:

• 6 pieces using pattern B

From brown fabric, cut:

• 6 pieces using pattern B

• 1 circle using pattern A

From tan fabric, cut:

• 1 square 13″ × 13″. After you are done with the appliqué work, trim to 12½″.

Newspaper Archive

Appeared in *The Kansas City Star* on June 4, 1952 (block #908) and as Old-Fashioned Wagon Wheels on June 20, 1955 (block #954)

From 1952: Original size: 11″, pieced and appliquéd. The design is from Mrs. Dessie Walters of Route 3, Pawnee, Oklahoma, daughter of a pioneer Oklahoma farmer. Develop your wagon wheels as you like them, in gay or somber tones, for truck or parade transport.

From 1955: Original block: 10½″, pieced. A subscriber of many years to *Weekly Star Farmer* and an enthusiastic quilt piecer, Mrs. T. A. Best of Locust Grove, Oklahoma, has offered this conception of an old-fashioned wagon wheel. She developed her block with alternate strips of one-tone blue and blue and red print on a white background. The red hub of her wheel is appliquéd with blue thread. Mrs. Best's choices are only suggested colors. The wedges may be alternate one-tones of different colors or one-tones alternating with prints that carry one or more of the one-tone wedge colors.

To Make the Block

1. Sew the pink and brown B pieces together, alternating the colors.

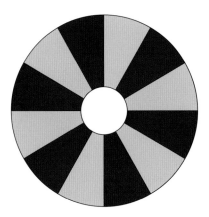

Press the outside edges under and appliqué to the background square.

2. Press the seam allowance of the center circle (pattern A) under and appliqué in place.

Trim the block to 12½˝. Although the diagram doesn't show it, you will need to leave a ¼˝ seam allowance around the outside edge of the block.

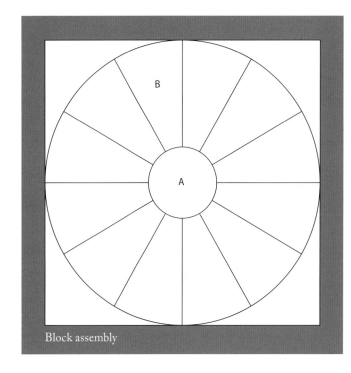

Block assembly

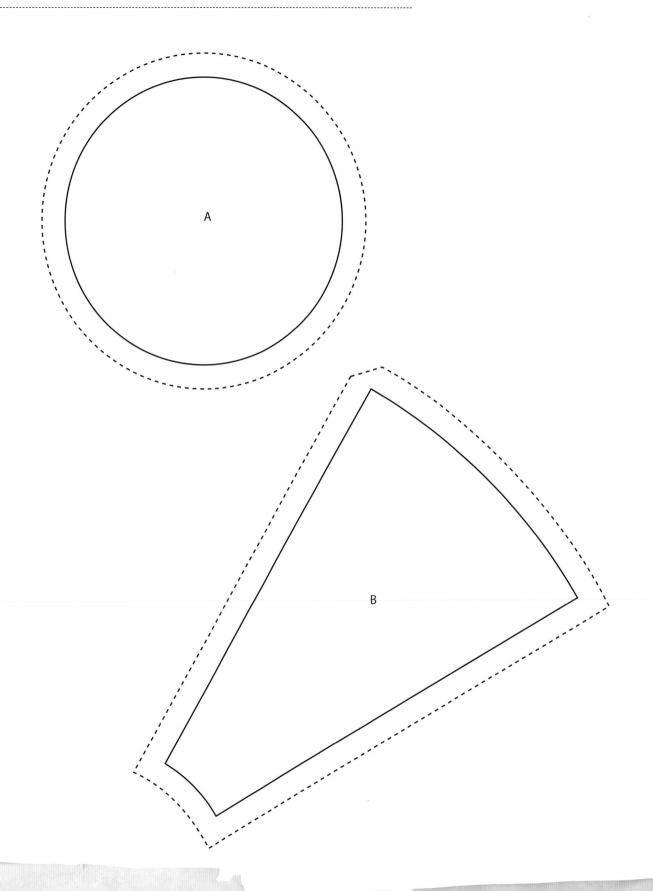

1953 Eight-Point Snowflake

Finished block: 12″ × 12″

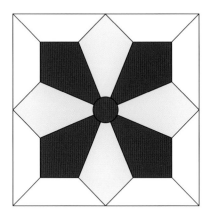

Fabric Needed

Light blue • Medium blue • Dark blue

Cutting Instructions

Use the Eight-Point Snowflake patterns (pages 211–212).

From light blue fabric, cut:

• 8 pieces using pattern A

From medium blue fabric, cut:

• 4 pieces using pattern B

From dark blue fabric, cut:

• 4 pieces using pattern C

• 1 circle using pattern D

Newspaper Archive

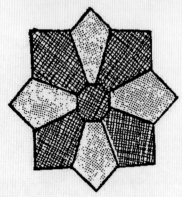

Appeared in *The Kansas City Star* on April 8, 1953 (block #921)

Alternate print and one-tone blocks, or an alternating arrangement of very small prints with checks or plaids, is pleasing for the Eight-Point Snowflake. The pattern is a contribution of Mrs. Bob Mullinax of Route 1, Farmington, Missouri.

To Make the Block

1. Sew the B and C pieces into 2 sets of 4. Don't sew all the way to the end of the seams, as they will be inset later.

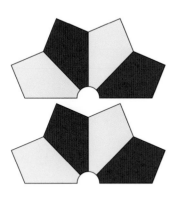

2. Join the 2 sets.

3. Add the A pieces. Sew in the directions of the arrows, then miter the seam where the 2 A pieces meet.

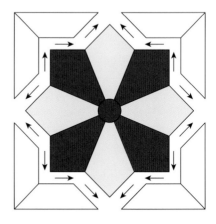

4. Appliqué the D circle in place to complete the block.

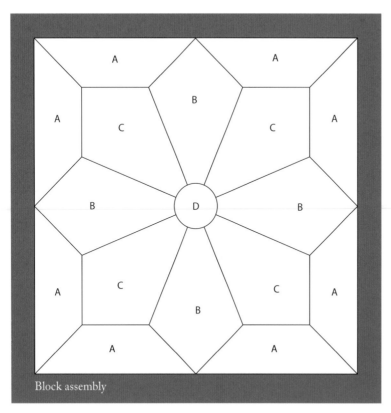

Block assembly

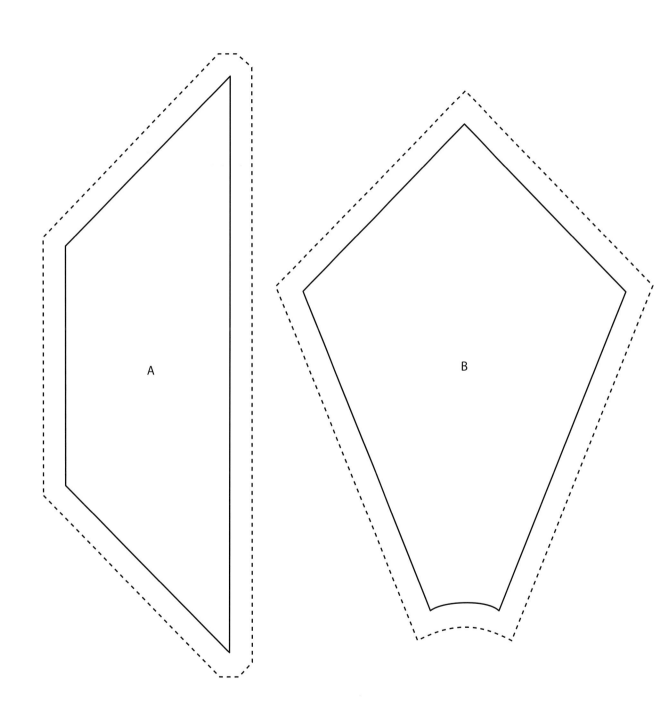

A

B

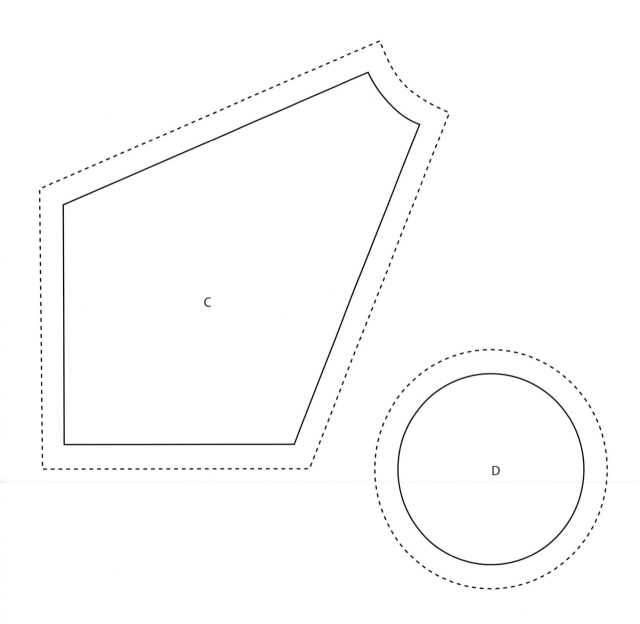

C

D

1954 Crystal Star

Finished block: 12″ × 12″

Fabric Needed

Red • Tan

Cutting Instructions

Use the Crystal Star patterns (page 215).

From red, cut:

• 6 squares 3⅞″ × 3⅞″ (or cut 12 triangles using pattern B)

From tan, cut:

• 4 squares 3½″ × 3½″ (pattern A)

• 6 squares 3⅞″ × 3⅞″ (or cut 12 triangles using pattern B)

Newspaper Archive

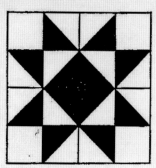

Appeared in *The Kansas City Star* on March 10, 1954 (block #937) and previously on June 16, 1934 (block #358)

From 1954: This is the Crystal Star quilt made by women of the Union Grove grange near Excello, Macon County, Missouri, which won first place in the 1953 Missouri grange quilt contest. It was presented recently to Mrs. Phil M. Donnelly, wife of the governor of Missouri. Mrs. Stanley Roebuck is home economics chairman of Union Grove grange. Other members of the grange are Mrs. Forrest Brock, Mrs. Marion Roebuck, Mrs. Gaylord Arnett, Mrs. Jesse Shannon, Mrs. Glen O'Toole, Miss Dollie Baker, Mrs. Annie Powell, Mrs. Arthur Richards, and Mrs. Leslie Brock. The pattern was clipped from *Weekly Star Farmer* 20 years ago.

From 1934: This is a pattern that the most inexperienced quiltmaker may use with confidence. Use any 2 colors desired. All seams are straight. Lemon yellow and green are good colors. Allow for seams. Next week, a difficult quilt for expert quilters will appear.

To Make the Block

1. Draw a line from corner to corner on the diagonal on the reverse side of the 3⅞″ tan squares. Place the tan square atop a red 3⅞″ square with right sides facing. Sew ¼″ on both sides of the drawn line. Use your rotary cutter and cut on the drawn line. Open the unit and press toward the darker fabric. This makes a half-square triangle unit. Each square will yield 2 half-square triangles. You need 12 for this block.

Sew a tan 3½″ square to a red and tan half-square triangle. Now add a half-square triangle unit. End the row with a tan square. Make 2 rows.

2. Now sew 4 half-square triangles together. Make 2 rows.

3. Sew the rows together to complete the block.

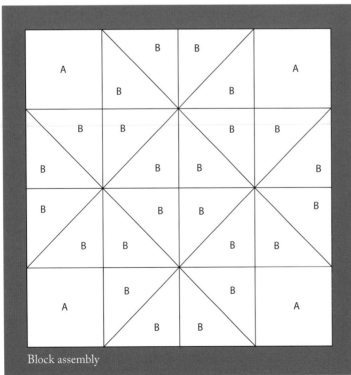

Block assembly

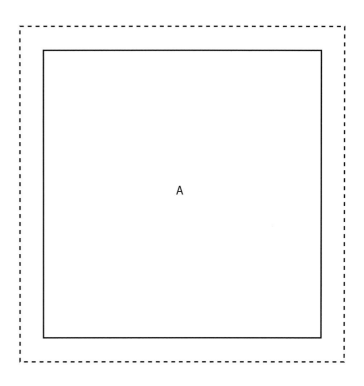

A

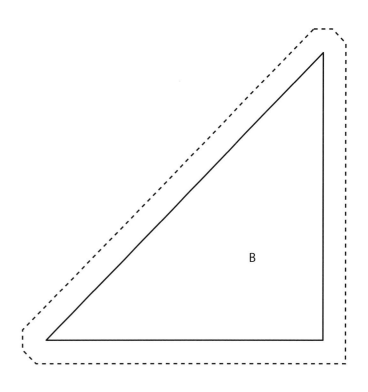

B

1954 Signature Quilt

Finished block: 6″ × 6″

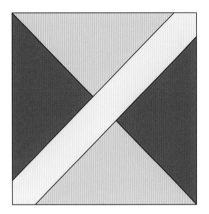

Fabric Needed

Brown • Pink • Light tan

Cutting Instructions

Use the Signature Quilt patterns (pages 218–219).

From brown fabric, cut:

• 2 triangles using pattern A

From pink fabric, cut:

• 2 triangles using pattern A

From light tan fabric, cut:

• 1 piece using pattern B

Newspaper Archive

Appeared in *The Kansas City Star* on February 10, 1954 (block #935)

Original size: 7½″. Everything to be desired for a Friendship Signature quilt is included in this pattern. There is a long white strip for the name, there are print blocks and one-tone pieces, with the choice of color left to the needlecrafter. The block was designed by Mrs. Clyde Offutt of Sleeper, Missouri, for her daughter, Miss Dixie L. Offutt.

To Make the Block

1. Sew a pink A piece to a brown A piece. Make 2.

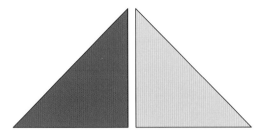

2. Sew a pink/brown unit to either side of the light tan B strip to complete the block.

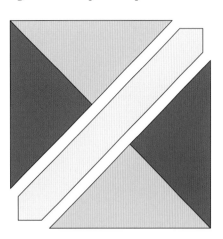

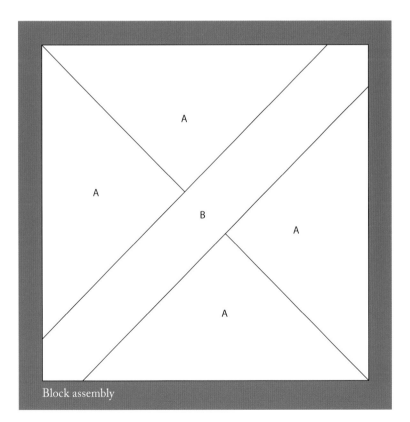

Block assembly

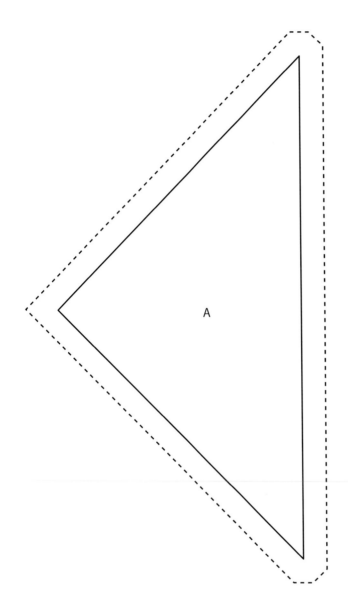

A

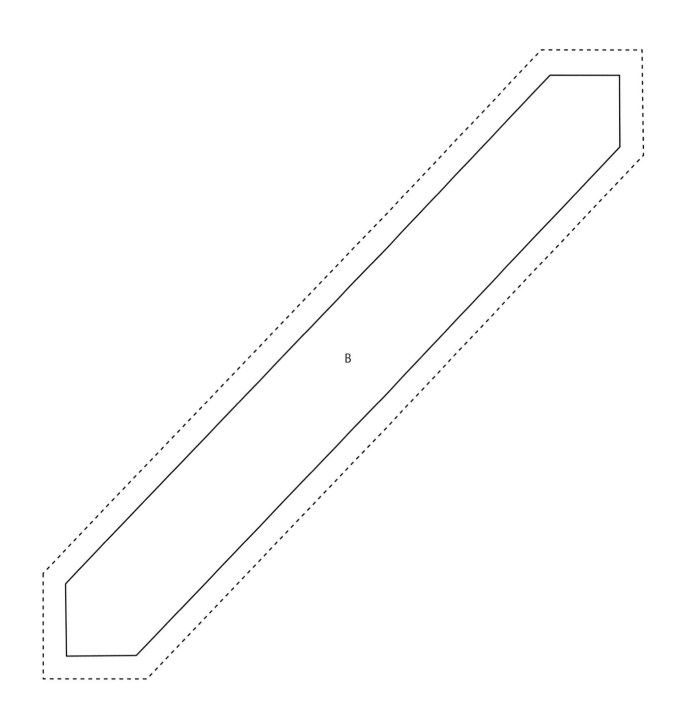

B

1955 Scrap Zigzag

Finished block: 12″ × 12″

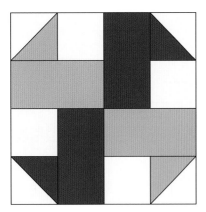

Fabric Needed

Green print • Brown print • Background

Cutting Instructions

Use the Scrap Zigzag patterns (pages 222–223). This block can also be made using a rotary cutter and ruler for the measured pieces.

From background fabric, cut:

- 2 squares 3⅞″ × 3⅞″ or use pattern A to cut 4 triangles
- 4 squares 3½″ × 3½″ (pattern B)

From brown print fabric, cut:

- 1 square 3⅞″ × 3⅞″ or use pattern A to cut 2 triangles
- 2 rectangles 3½″ × 6½″ (pattern C)

Newspaper Archive

Appeared in *The Kansas City Star* on October 26, 1955 (block #964)

Although the original design of this zigzag calls for a print and a one-tone, the color scheme could be varied by choosing 2 one-tone pieces harmonizing with the print. The pattern comes from Letha McBroom, Huntsville, Arkansas.

From green print fabric, cut:

- 1 square 3⅞″ × 3⅞″
- 2 rectangles 3½″ × 6½″

To Make the Block

1. Make 4 half-square triangle units. Draw a line from corner to corner on the reverse side of the 3⅞″ background squares. Place one background square atop the brown print 3⅞″ square and the other atop the green print square with right sides facing. Sew ¼″ on either side of the line. Using your rotary cutter, cut along the drawn line. Open the units and press toward the dark fabric. If you would prefer, you can make your half-square triangles by sewing a background A triangle to the brown and green.

2. Sew each of the half-square triangles to a background square.

3. Sew these units to a rectangle.

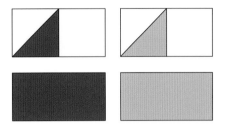

4. Sew the 4 quadrants together to complete the block.

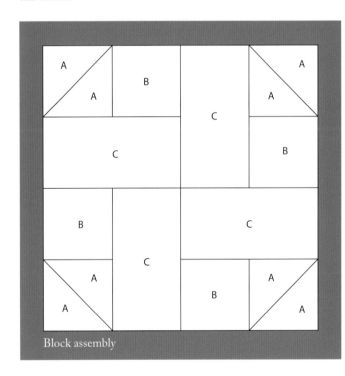

Block assembly

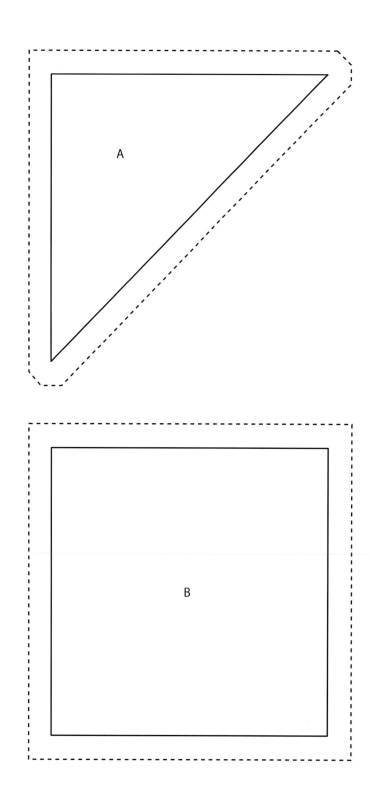

C

1955 Many Roads to the White House

Finished block: 12″ × 12″

Fabric Needed

Cream • Brown print • Tan

Cutting Instructions

Use the Many Roads to the White House patterns (pages 226–227).

From cream fabric, cut:

• 8 triangles using pattern C

From brown print, cut:

• 8 pieces using pattern B

From tan fabric, cut:

• 4 pieces using pattern A

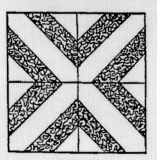

To Make the Block

1. Sew a cream C piece to a brown print B piece. Make 8.

2. Sew a B-C unit to both sides of a tan A piece. Make 4.

3. Sew the 4 quadrants of the block together.

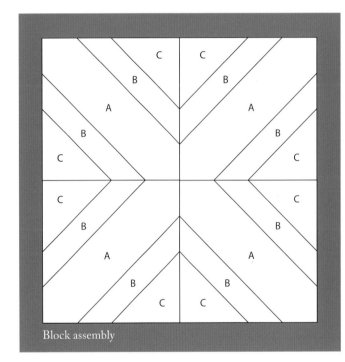

Block assembly

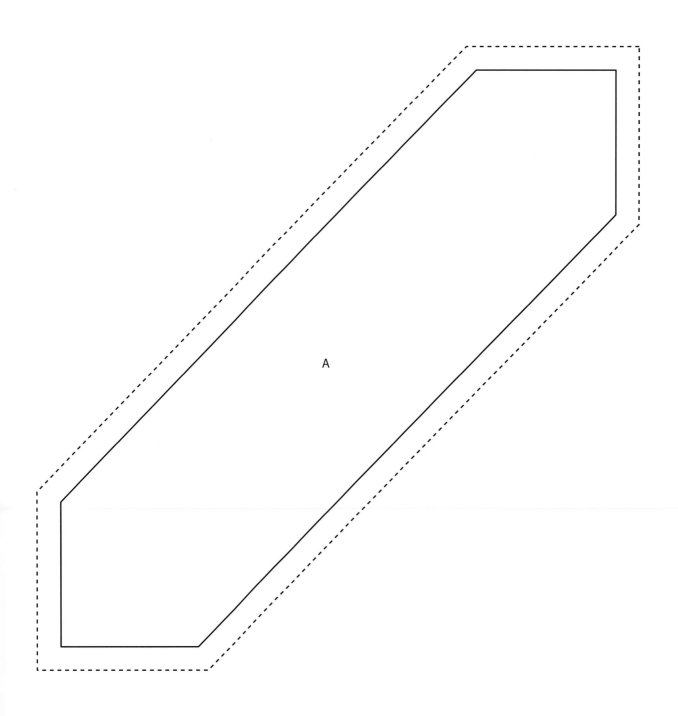

A

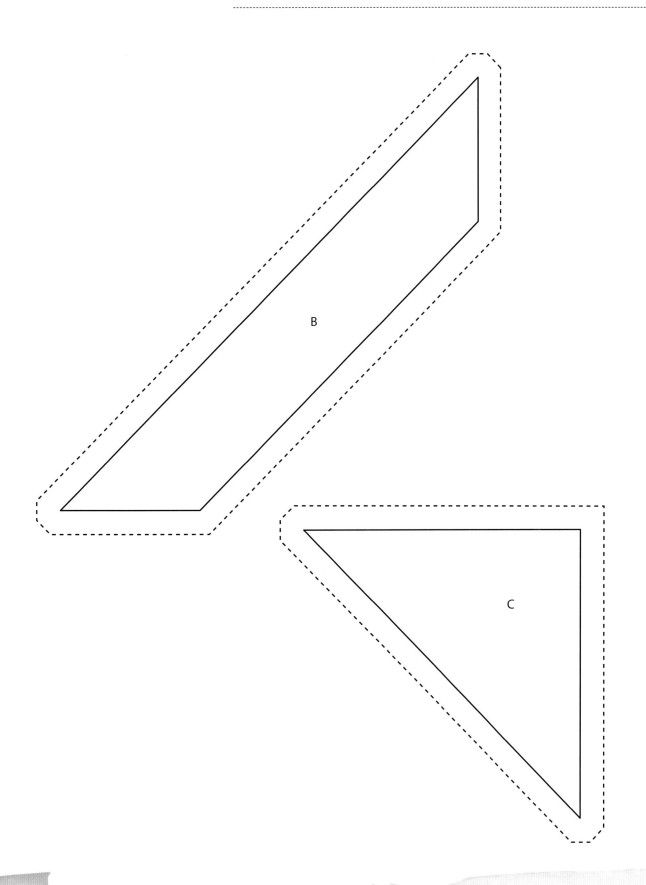

B

C

1955 Rose Cross

Finished block: 15″ × 15″

Fabric Needed

Background fabric • Pink • Rose
Green • Yellow

Cutting Instructions

Use the Rose Cross patterns (pages 229–230). This block can also be made using a rotary cutter and ruler for the measured pieces.

NOTE: Add ⅛″–¼″ seam allowances to all pieces.

From pink fabric, cut:

• 4 flower buds

• 1 inner flower

From green fabric, cut:

• 16 leaves

• 4 calyx

• 4 bias strips ½″ × 4″ for stems

Newspaper Archive

Appeared in *The Kansas City Star* on September 14, 1955 (block #80)

Original size: 15″. Appliqué quilting is one of the most popular branches of the art and it is for lovers of appliqué that the Rose Crown is offered. Unlike piecing, appliqué offers diversifications and embellishments. The patterns may be made just as elaborate as the maker chooses and her originality has more chance to assert itself. This pattern shows a decorative combination of a cross motif and a foundation rose pattern. The colors are optional, but there is no prettier combination than the ones suggested here in yellow, rose, and pink, with the leaves developed in green. Of all the patterns developed from the rose as a central foundation, this is one of the most charming.

From rose fabric, cut:

• 1 outer flower

From background fabric, cut:

• 1 square 16½″ × 16½″

From yellow fabric, cut:

• 1 flower center

To Make the Block

1. Fold the background fabric in quarters from corner to corner on the diagonal and press the creases in lightly for placement purposes.

2. Prepare the appliqué pieces using the appliqué method of your choice.

3. Pin the appliqué elements in place and stitch.

4. When you are done with the appliqué work, press the block and trim to 15½″.

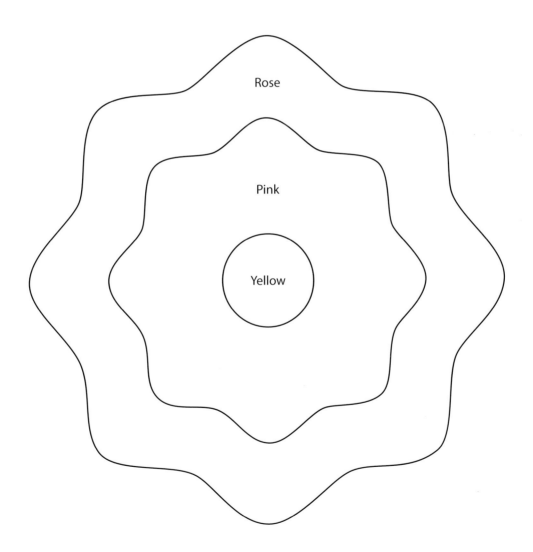

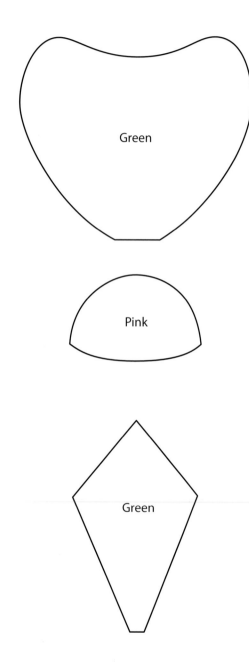

Green

Pink

Green

1956 Rising Sun

Finished block: 12″ × 12″

Fabric Needed

Red • Blue • Tan

Cutting Instructions

Use the Rising Sun patterns (pages 234–235). This challenging block uses a combination of paper piecing and regular piecing. For pattern A, it might be helpful to cut out a triangle template that is ½″ larger on all 3 sides. Notice that the triangles on each end of the strip are smaller.

From red fabric, cut:

- 6 pieces using pattern C
- 1 circle using pattern D
- 24 triangles: Measure one of the triangles on paper-piecing pattern A.

From blue fabric, cut:

- 6 pieces using pattern C
- 28 triangles: Measure one of the triangles on paper-piecing pattern A.

From tan fabric, cut:

- 4 pieces using pattern B

Newspaper Archive

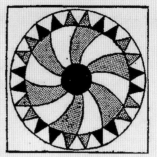

Appeared in *The Kansas City Star* on September 12, 1956 (block #994) and previously on February 2, 1929 (block #20) and September 26, 1936 (block #473)

From 1956: The Rising Sun, reputed to be one of the oldest patterns of American quilt-makers, was a pattern reproduced in *Weekly Star Farmer* years ago. Emma W. Swicegood of Tulsa, Oklahoma, sent it from her collection, thinking today's quiltmakers might be interested.

From 1929: This is a quilt pattern for which many requests have been received. It is rather an intricate pattern, but will not daunt the quilter who aspires to a design that is both lovely and unusual. All the patterns given here are for one block. Make cardboard cutting patterns, and mark lightly around them onto material. Then cut a seam larger all around and sew back to the pencil lines. First piece 4 small triangles, 2 white and 2 in color, into a block which in turn is sewed to the curved block. When 12 of these are pieced sew the long seams which make it into a wheel. The "hub" is creased around and appliquéd to center. This whole wheel, or sun, may either be appliquéd on a 12″ square, or pieced in with the 4 white corner blocks as shown in the pattern. Flame red and orange with white, unbleached, or yellow muslin are appropriate for this pattern.

From 1936: The Rising Sun is one of the early colonial patterns which is now revived by quilt fans. Choose your own colors and allow for seams. This design is sent by Mrs. Cecelia Becker of Owensville, Missouri, an ardent quilt fan.

To Make the Block

1. Paper piece the 4 A sections. The inner triangles will be red and the outer triangles will be blue.

2. Sew the red and blue C pieces together, alternating the colors.

3. Press the seam allowance under the center circle and appliqué it to the center of the block.

4. Fold the center of the block in half and lightly press a crease in the fold.

Fold.

5. Fold the block in half again and lightly press creases in the fold.

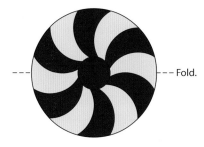

Fold.

6. Sew the 4 A sections together leaving the last seam open.

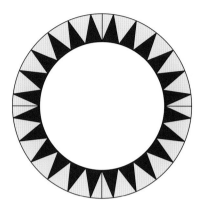

8. Sew the 4 tan B pieces together, leaving the last seam open. Pin to the inside of the block, being careful to match the seam allowances. Sew in place and close up the last seam.

7. Match up the seam allowances and the pressed creases. Pin in place. Pin the outer circle all the way around the inner circle, being very careful to match where the seams intersect. Stitch together. Close up the last A seam.

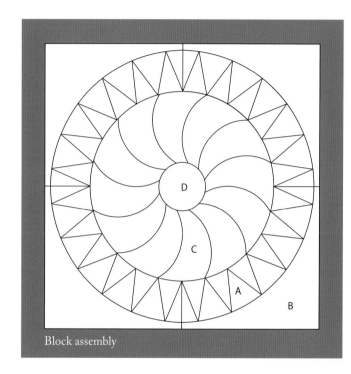

Block assembly

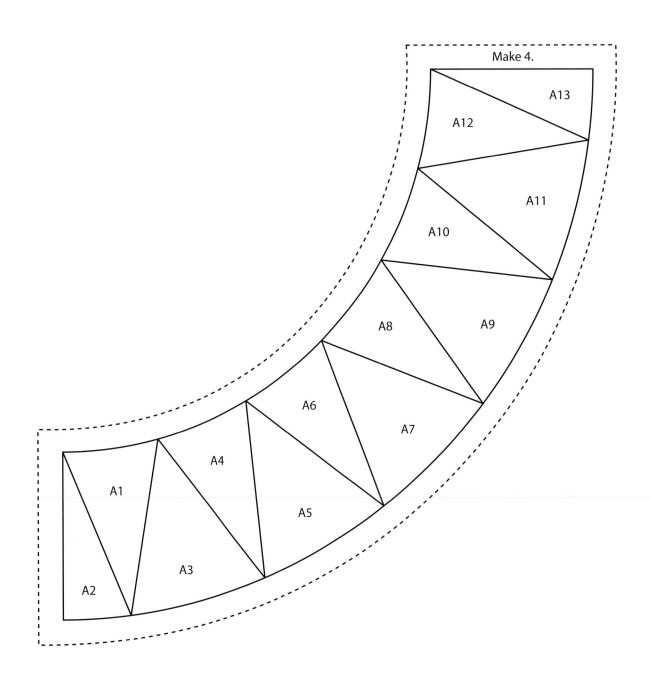

Make 4.

A13

A12

A11

A10

A9

A8

A7

A6

A5

A4

A3

A1

A2

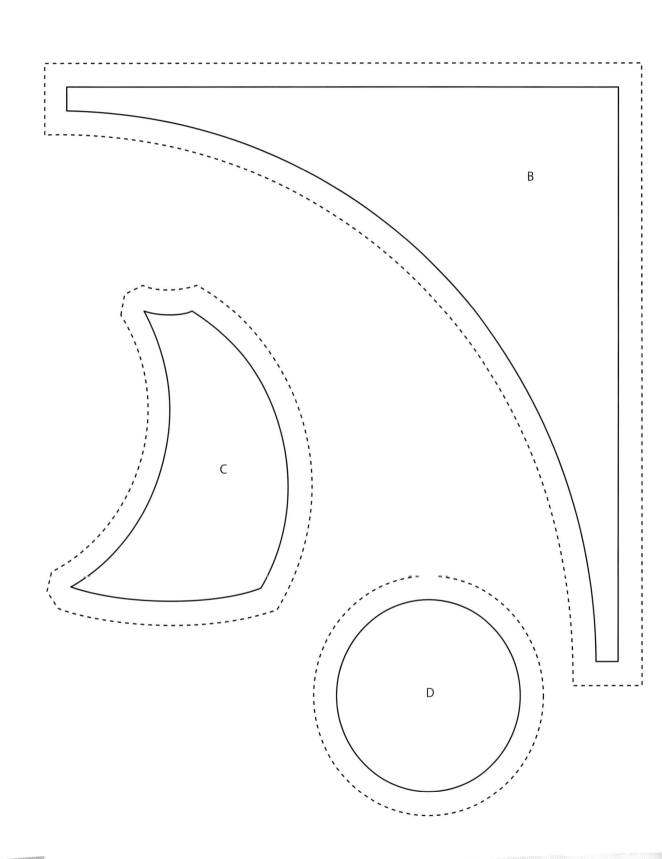

B

C

D

1957 Oklahoma's Square Dance

Finished block: 12″ × 12″

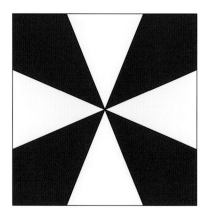

Fabric Needed

Dark blue • Light shirting

Cutting Instructions

Use the Oklahoma's Square Dance patterns (pages 238–239).

From dark blue fabric, cut:

• 4 pieces using pattern A

From light shirting, cut:

• 4 triangles using pattern B

Newspaper Archive

Appeared in *The Kansas City Star* on October 30, 1957 (block #1013)

Original size: 6½″, pieced. An imaginative conception of the square dance as it is done in Oklahoma is depicted by Emma W. Swicegood of Tulsa, Oklahoma.

To Make the Block

1. Sew the A and B pieces together into 2 sets of 4, alternating the colors.

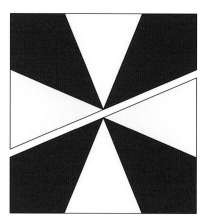

2. Sew the 2 sets of 4 together on the diagonal to complete the block.

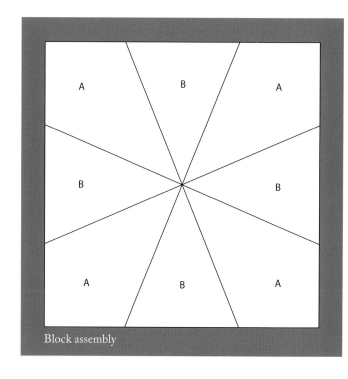

Block assembly

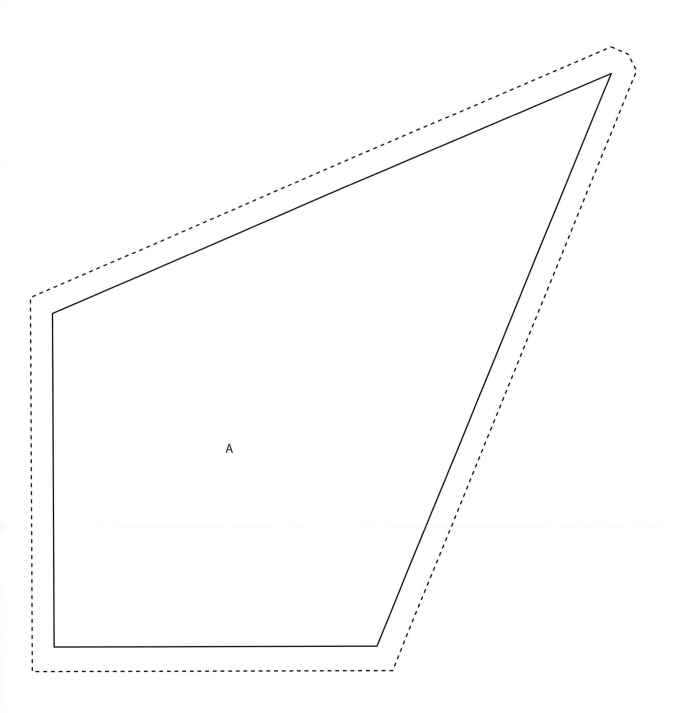

A

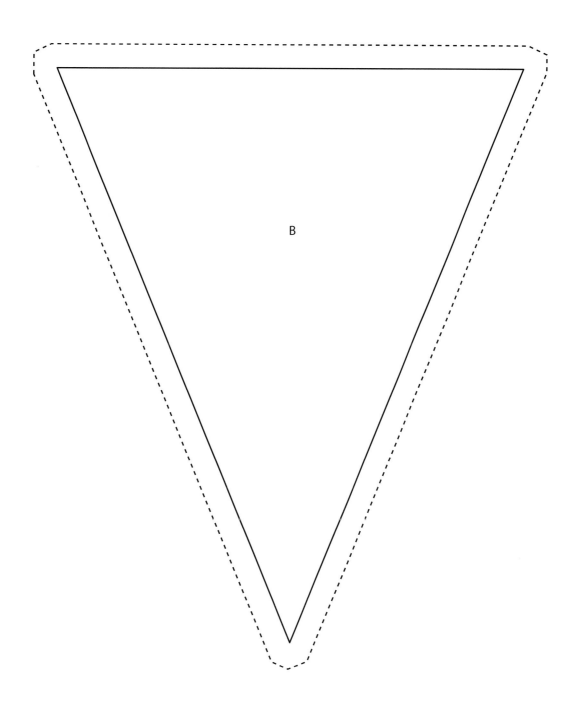

B

1958 Flying Colors

Finished block: 12″ × 12″

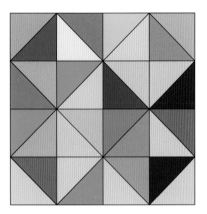

Fabric Needed

Use this as a "stash buster" and get rid of those small leftover fabric scraps. Use scraps of all colors, but each must be at least a 3⅞″ square or large enough to cut triangles using the pattern provided.

Cutting Instructions

Use the Flying Colors pattern (page 241). This block can also be made using a rotary cutter and ruler.

If you use the pattern:

- Cut 32 triangles, using dark, medium, and light fabric scraps. Make half-square triangle units by sewing the triangles together along the diagonal. Open the units and press toward the darkest fabric. You need to make 16 half-square triangles.

Newspaper Archive

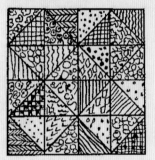

Appeared in *The Kansas City Star* on November 5, 1958 (block #1027)

The title, Flying Colors, was given to this quilt block by its designer, Mrs. Mart Ledbetter of Witter, Arkansas, because she pieced it from flying bits or leftovers from other quilts.

If you use a rotary cutter:

- Cut 16 squares 3⅞″ × 3⅞″. Draw a line on the diagonal from corner to corner on the reverse side of the lightest colored squares. Place a light square atop a dark square and sew ¼″ on either side of the line. Use your rotary cutter and cut on the line, open each unit, and press toward the darkest fabric.

To Make the Block

1. Sew 4 half-square triangles together in a row. Make 4 rows.

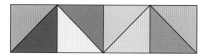

2. Sew the 4 rows together to complete the block.

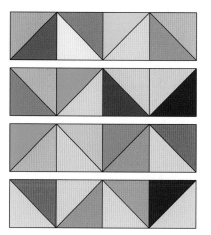

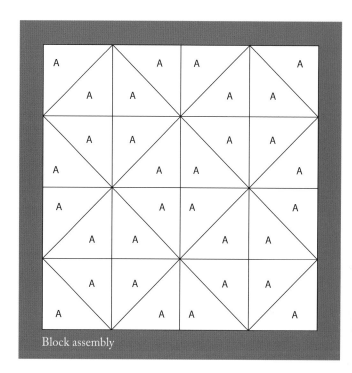

Block assembly

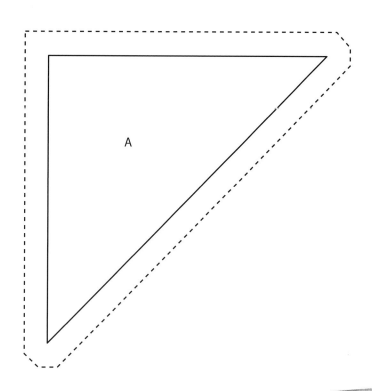

1958 Dogwood Blossom

Finished block: 12″ × 12″

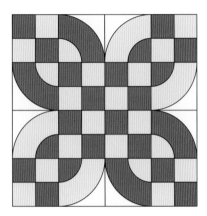

Fabric Needed

Dark pink • Light pink print • Cream

Cutting Instructions

Use the Dogwood Blossom patterns (page 244). This block can also be made using a rotary cutter and ruler for the measured pieces.

From dark pink fabric, cut:

• 16 squares 2″ × 2″ (pattern A)

• 4 pieces using pattern D

• 4 pieces using pattern C

Appeared in *The Kansas City Star* on September 17, 1958 (block #1025)

Original size: 16½″. This design represents the impression of Mrs. Gust Hesemann of Route 1, Owensville, Missouri, of a wild dogwood blossom. In keeping with the delicate coloring of this flower, pastel colors are suggested for the individual pieces.

From light pink print fabric, cut:

• 16 squares 2″ × 2″ (pattern A)

• 4 pieces using pattern D

• 4 pieces using pattern C

From cream fabric, cut:

• 8 pieces using pattern B

To Make the Block

1. Sew the dark pink and light pink print A squares together to make four-patch units. Make 8.

2. Stitch a cream B piece to a dark pink D piece. Add a light pink print C piece. Make 4.

3. Stitch a cream B piece to a light pink print D piece. Add a dark pink C piece. Make 4.

4. Stitch the units together as shown. You will have 2 quadrants of the block that have dark pink in the curved pieces and 2 that will have light pink print.

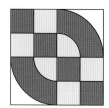 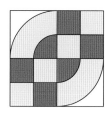

5. Sew the quadrants together to complete the block.

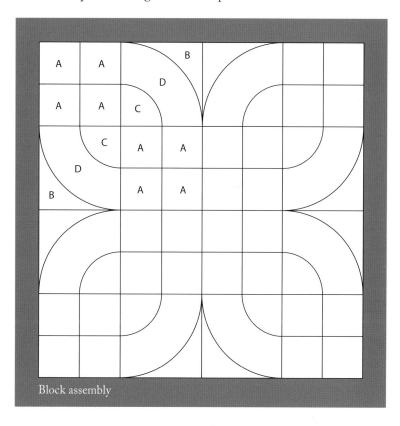

Block assembly

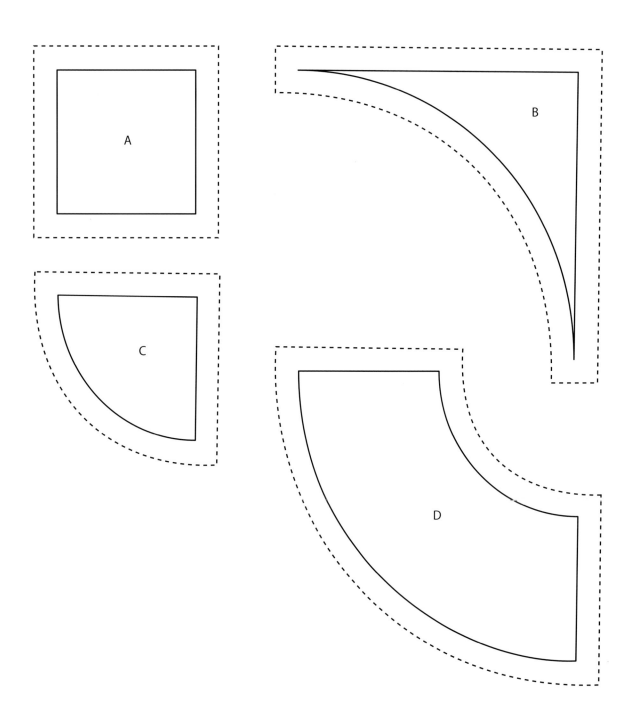

1959 Carnival Time

Finished block: 12″ × 12″

Fabric Needed

Red • Tan

Cutting Instructions

Use the Carnival Time patterns (pages 247–248).

NOTE: This block is far easier to make when paper pieced. Cut all the pieces ½″ larger than needed all the way around each piece. I've also found I like Carol Doak's Foundation Paper (by C&T Publishing) for this method better than anything else I've tried. Another hint: Use double-sided tape to hold the first piece of fabric in place. Leave the paper on until the entire block is sewn together.

From red fabric:

• Cut the pieces for the following positions:

A1 – A3 – A5

B1 – B3 – B5

From tan fabric:

• Cut the pieces for the following positions:

A2 – A4

B2 – B4

Newspaper Archive

Appeared in *The Kansas City Star* on September 9, 1959 (block #1036)

This fascinating block may be developed in a wide variety of color teaming. The outer circle would be particularly engaging in 2 alternating, red and blue, for instance, with the inner circle cut from one of those colors. It is suggested that the prints be of small design. The contributor of the design is Mrs. May Bess of Route 1, Poplar Bluff, Missouri.

To Make the Block

1. Sew the pieces to the paper in the order printed on each pattern. You'll need to print out and make 4 A units and 4 B units.

Sew the A units to the B units along the diagonal. Each A-B unit comprises one-fourth of the block.

2. Sew the 4 A-B units together to complete the block. Don't forget to wait until all your blocks are sewn together into a completed top before you remove the paper.

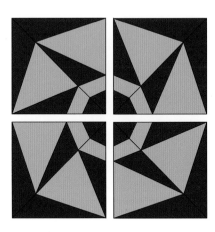

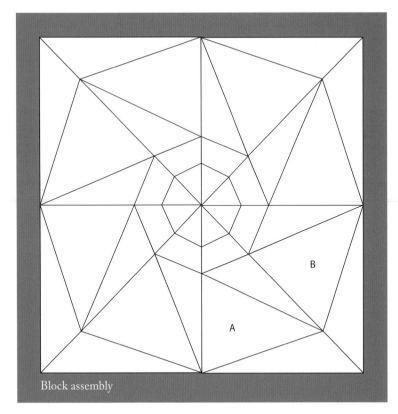

Block assembly

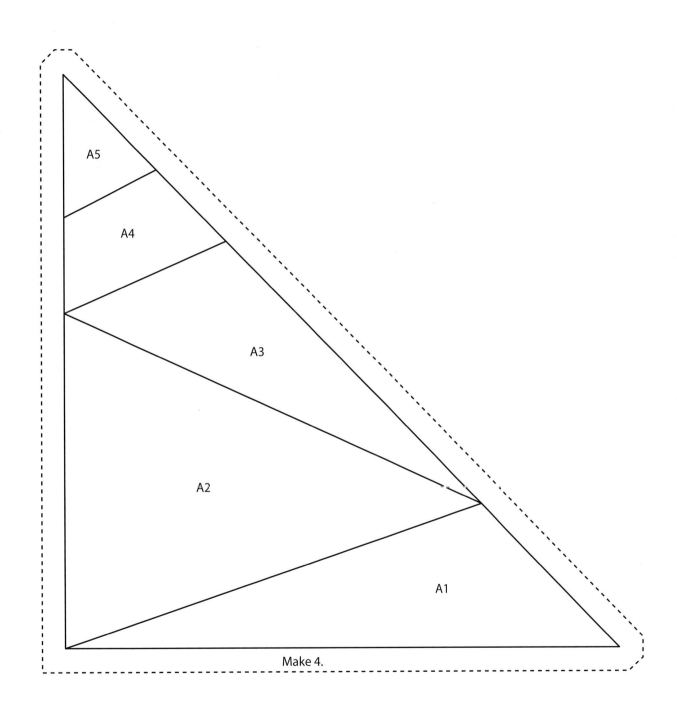

A5

A4

A3

A2

A1

Make 4.

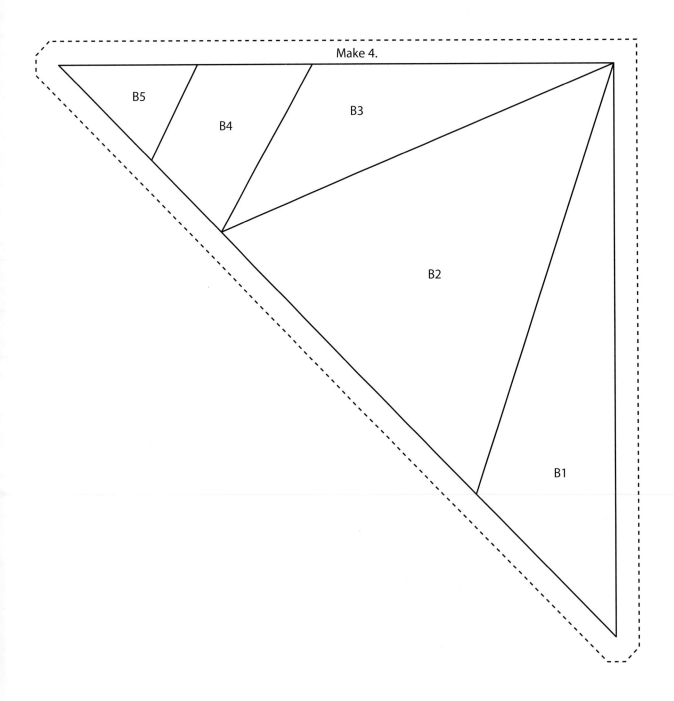

Make 4.

B5

B4

B3

B2

B1

1960s

See the Rain Drop block (page 250).

Right out of the Blue, designed and stitched by Barbara Dahl of Bellingham, Washington; quilted by Janice Howell of Everson, Washington

1960 Rain Drop

Finished block: *6″ × 6″*

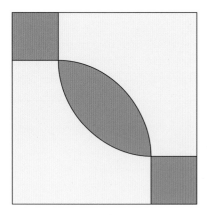

Fabric Needed

Pale blue • Medium blue

Cutting Instructions

Use the Rain Drop patterns (page 252).

From pale blue fabric, cut:

• 2 pieces using pattern B

From medium blue fabric, cut:

• 1 piece using pattern C

• 2 squares using pattern A

Newspaper Archive

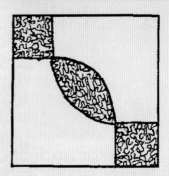

Appeared in *The Kansas City Star* on March 16, 1960 (block #1045)

A combination of 1 solid color and 3 pieces of small print create the Rain Drop. Hazel Mullinax of Farmington, Missouri, who offers the pattern, says this is a very easy block to put together.

To Make the Block

1. Sew a light blue B piece to the medium C piece.

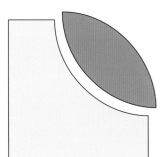

2. Sew the medium blue A squares to the remaining B piece.

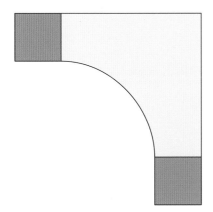

3. Stitch the 2 units together to complete the block.

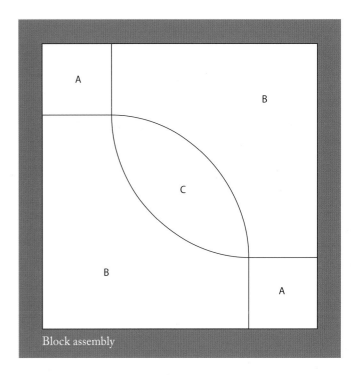

Block assembly

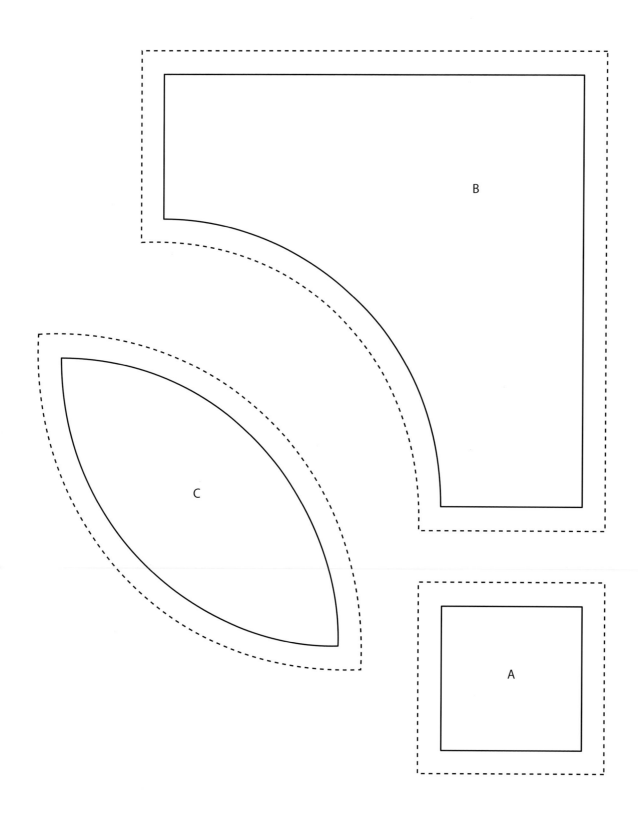

1960 Rope and Anchor

Finished block: 9″ × 9″

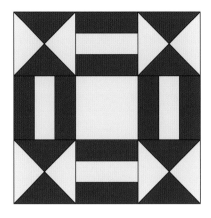

Fabric Needed

Brown • Blue print

Cutting Instructions

Use the Rope and Anchor patterns (page 255). This block can also be made using a rotary cutter and ruler.

From brown fabric, cut:

• 2 squares 4¼″ × 4¼″. Cut each square from corner to corner twice on the diagonal, or use pattern A.

• 8 rectangles 1½″ × 3½″ or use pattern B

From blue fabric, cut:

• 2 squares 4¼″ × 4¼″. Cut each square from corner to corner twice on the diagonal, or use pattern A.

• 4 rectangles 1½″ × 3½″ or use pattern B

• 1 square 3½″ × 3½″

Newspaper Archive

Appeared in *The Kansas City Star* on May 11, 1960 (block #1048) and previously as Broken Dish on August 21, 1937 (block #516).

From 1960: Original size: 8¼″. This maritime theme, the Rope and Anchor, is most effective when developed in 2 colors. Like any marquetry skill is required in cutting the pieces and in putting them together to preserve the straight lines. The design is an offering of Amelia Lampton of Aguilar, Colorado.

From 1937: Original size: 9″ This may be in any plain color and white to suit the room in which it is to be used. The Broken Dish is also called Rope and Anchor design. It is sent by Mrs. A. L. Stimpson of Galt, Missouri.

To Make the Block

1. Sew a blue triangle to a brown triangle. Make 2 and sew them together. You now have a quarter-square triangle unit. Make 4, one for each corner of the block.

2. Sew the rectangles together. Make 4.

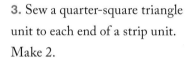

3. Sew a quarter-square triangle unit to each end of a strip unit. Make 2.

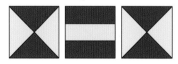

4. Sew a strip unit to either side of the blue square.

5. Sew the 3 rows together to complete the block.

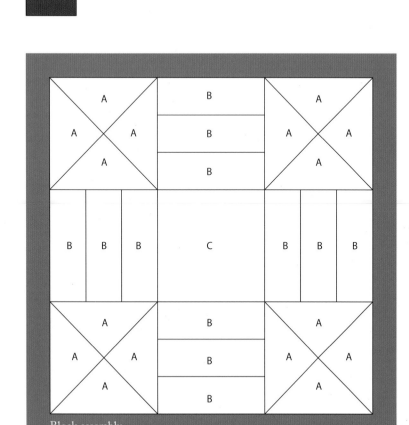

Block assembly

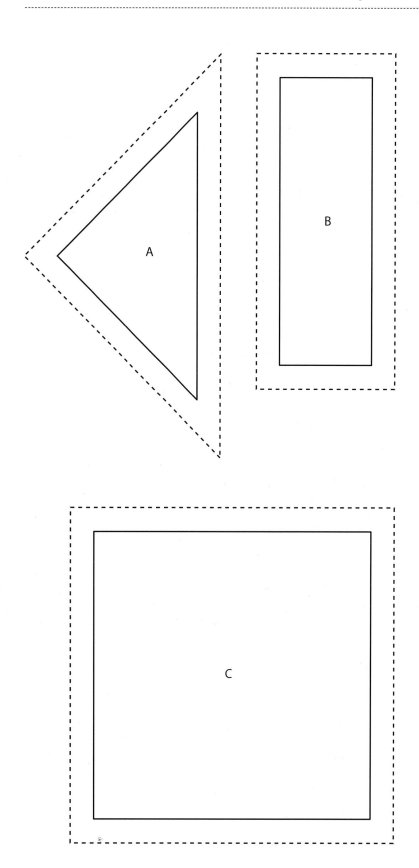

1961 Bell

Finished block: *6″ × 6″*

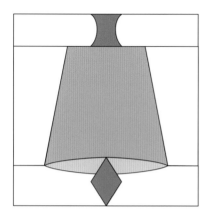

Fabric Needed

Light blue • Light medium blue
Medium blue • Dark medium blue

Cutting Instructions

Use the Bell patterns (pages 258–259).

From light blue fabric, cut:

• 2 pieces using pattern A

• 1 piece using patterns C, D, E and F

From dark medium blue fabric, cut:

• 1 piece using pattern B

• 1 piece using pattern J

From medium blue fabric, cut:

• 1 piece using pattern G

From light medium blue fabric, cut:

• 1 piece using pattern H

• 1 piece using pattern I

Newspaper Archive

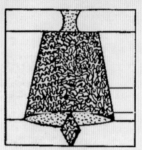

Appeared in *The Kansas City Star*
on March 15, 1961 (block #1058)

Listening to the tone of the bells on the cows as they came home late in the afternoon from grazing on the open range inspired the mother of Mrs. Mae Dees of Route 1, Coldwater, Missouri, to design this bell for a quilt block. Mrs. Dees says the pattern was designed at least 60 years ago. She recently found the tattered paper on which it was drawn, reconstructed it, and mailed it to *Weekly Star Farmer*. It immediately impresses one as appropriate for members of any of the CowBelle organizations. Depending upon the metal chosen by a state group, the bell may be developed in copper or silver tones. A small print is suggested for the bell. The clapper is appliquéd.

To Make the Block

1. Sew a light blue A piece to each side of the B piece.

2. Sew the light blue F piece and the light blue C piece to piece G.

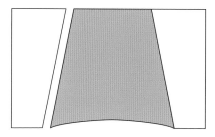

3. Sew piece H to E and I to D.

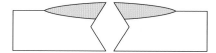

4. Stitch to either side of J.

5. Sew the 3 rows together to complete the block.

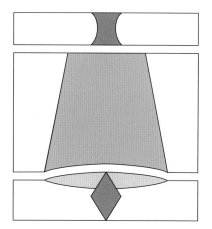

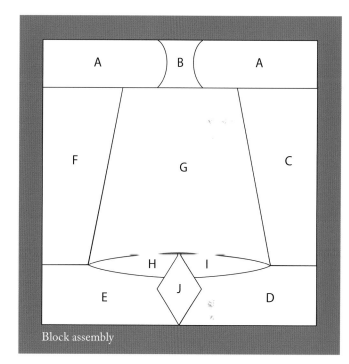

Block assembly

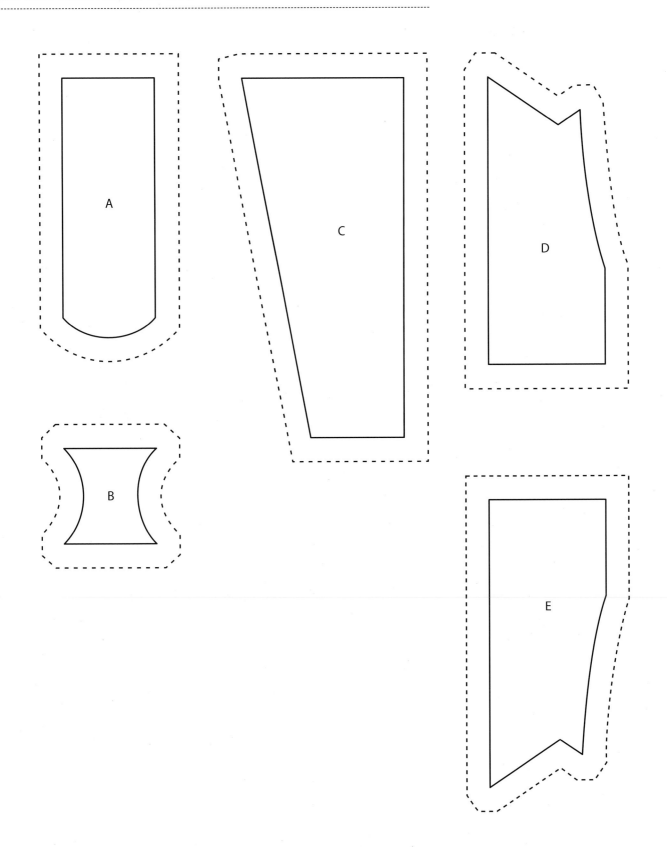

A

C

D

B

E

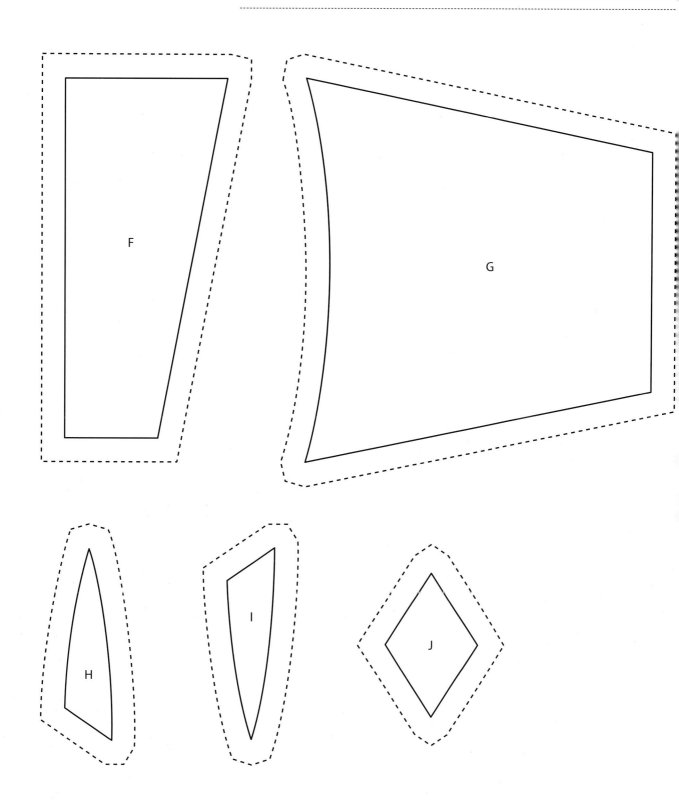

The Kansas City Star Quilts Sampler

Finished quilt: 87½″ × 93″ • **Finished blocks:** 6″ × 6″, 9″ × 9″, and 12″ × 12″

The Kansas City Star Quilts Sampler, designed by Debbie Rodgers with technical support by Linda Johnson; pieced by Helen Frost, Linda Johnson, Debbie Rodgers, Gailen Runge, and Teresa Stroin; quilted by Susan Dillinger, 2018

When we started to pull the Kansas City Star blocks to include in this book, it quickly became apparent that we wanted to sew them up to see them come alive in fabric. But how to do that?

The blocks as presented in the newspaper were different sizes and we wanted to honor the original. We decided to reduce and enlarge the blocks as necessary to create a dynamic sampler while leaving the blocks in their original sizes in the book. We designed a sampler featuring three sizes of blocks: 6″ × 6″, 9″ × 9″, and 12″ × 12″ and included sashing to add structure and even up the spacing on the rows.

Once we had the plan for the number of blocks we needed in each size, we picked which blocks would be which and what would go where. And we estimated yardage. The fabric in this quilt is Blue Sky by Edyta Sitar, Bijoux by Kathy Hall, and Clotted Creams and Caramels by Di Ford-Hall, generously donated by Andover Fabrics.

We printed out the blocks at their new size (enlarging or reducing as needed). For blocks that did or could use templates, we traced the shapes and created templates. For blocks where rotary cutting and traditional piecing made sense, we measured the finished pieces in the new pattern and added seam allowances as appropriate.

Then we paired each block with chunks of appropriate fabrics and divided them between ourselves and our additional block sewists: Helen Frost, Gailen Runge, and Teresa Stroin. We couldn't have done it without their help!

Because we have conveniences that were not available to the original block designers, we sometimes used fusible web to appliqué shapes that might have been hand pieced, and rotary cut and strip pieced sections that would have been stitched one patch to another. You may choose to do this or you may stick with the traditional methods for these traditional blocks!

We sewed the blocks together with sashing and borders and dropped it off at our quilter's. Susan Dillinger performed magic with her machine and really added wonderful details to the top.

And that's it!

We'd love to see your sampler or other project featuring these blocks. Post them on Instagram and tag *@ctpublishing*.

If you, too, would like to create a sampler featuring all the blocks in this book, see the pages that follow for specific instructions.

Warm regards,

Debbie Rodgers and Linda Johnson
Technical Editors, C&T Publishing

Yardage Estimates

We used a wide variety of fabrics, so the yardage below is the total for several different prints within each color. The yardage is based on 42˝ usable fabric width.

Cream: 5 yards

Tan: 5¾ yards

Apricot: ⅞ yard

Peach: 1¼ yards

Rust: 1⅜ yards

Light blue: ⅞ yard

Medium blue: 1⅝ yards

Dark blue: 3⅛ yards

Sashing, borders, and binding: 4 yards

Backing: 9 yards

Batting: 96˝ × 101˝

Cutting for Sashing, Borders, and Binding

LOF = length of fabric • WOF = width of fabric

- Cut 2 strips 2½˝ × 89˝ along the LOF and set aside for side borders.

- Cut 2 strips 2½˝ × 87½˝ along the LOF and set aside for top and bottom borders.

- Cut 7 strips 2˝ × 83½˝ along the LOF and set aside for horizontal sashing.

- Cut 6 strips 2¾˝ × WOF; subcut 16 strips 2¾˝ × 12½˝.

- Cut 1 strip 2½˝ × WOF; subcut 4 strips 2½˝ × 12½˝, using the remaining 2¾˝ strip also.

- Cut 1 strip 2¼˝ × WOF; subcut 4 strips 2¼˝ × 9½˝.

- Cut 3 strips 2˝ × WOF; subcut 10 strips 2˝ × 9½˝.

- Cut 3 strips 1½˝ × WOF; subcut into 22 strips 1½˝ × 6½˝, using the remaining 2˝ strip also.

- Cut 9 strips 2˝ × WOF for ¼˝ double-fold binding.

Construction

1. Sew together 24 blocks 6˝ × 6˝, 16 blocks 9˝ × 9˝, and 24 blocks 12˝ × 12˝. To help you create the blocks, see the Resizing Chart (at right).

2. With the 6˝ × 6˝ blocks, create 2 rows of 12 blocks, joined with sashing strips 1½˝ × 6½˝. You will need 11 sashing strips per row.

3. With the 9˝ × 9˝ blocks, create 2 rows of 8 blocks each. The first and last pairs of blocks in each row are joined with 2¼˝ × 9½˝ strips. The remaining center blocks are joined with 2˝ × 9½˝ sashing strips. You will need 2 strips 2¼˝ × 9½˝ and 5 strips 2˝ × 9½˝ per row.

Resizing Chart

Enlarge or reduce the beginning blocks by the listed percentages.

Beginning block*	To make 6˝ × 6˝	To make 9˝ × 9˝	To make 12˝ × 12˝
5˝ × 5˝	120%	180%	240%
6˝ × 6˝	100%	150%	200%
7½˝ × 7½˝	80%	120%	160%
9˝ × 9˝	67%	100%	133%
10˝ × 10˝	60%	90%	120%
11˝ × 11˝	55%	82%	109%
11⅞˝ × 11⅞˝	51%	76%	101%
12˝ × 12˝	50%	75%	100%
15˝ × 15˝	40%	60%	80%
16½˝ × 16½˝	36%	55%	73%

All block measurements are finished sizes.

4. With the 12″ × 12″ blocks, create 4 rows of 6 blocks each. The center 2 blocks are joined with a 2½″ × 12½″ sashing strip. The remaining blocks are joined with 2¾″ × 12½″ sashing strips. You will need 1 strip 2½″ × 12½″ and 4 strips 2¾″ × 12½″ per row.

5. Following the quilt assembly diagram, sew the rows and horizontal sashing together.

6. Sew the 2½″ × 89″ strips to both sides of the quilt. Then sew the 2½″ × 87½″ to the top and bottom of the quilt.

7. Layer, quilt as desired, and bind.

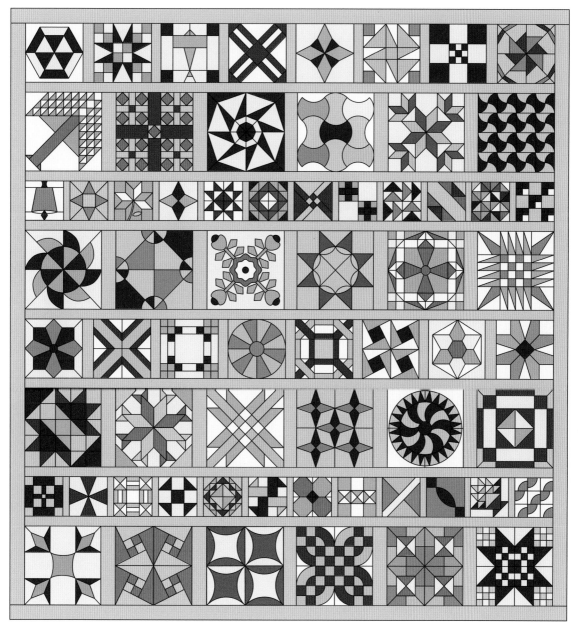

Quilt assembly

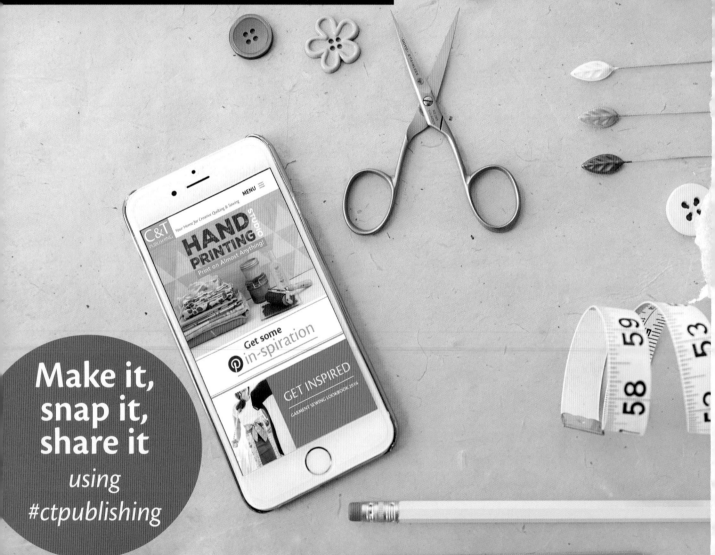

Want even more creative content?

Go to ctpub.com/offer

& sign up to receive our gift to you!

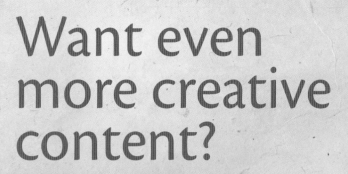

Make it, snap it, share it *using* #ctpublishing